Dr. Major W. Von Scherff

THE NEW TACTICS OF INFANTRY

(studies in.)

Dr. Major W. Von Scherff

THE NEW TACTICS OF INFANTRY
(studies in.)

ISBN/EAN: 9783741163968

Manufactured in Europe, USA, Canada, Australia, Japa

Cover: Foto ©ninafisch / pixelio.de

Manufactured and distributed by brebook publishing software
(www.brebook.com)

Dr. Major W. Von Scherff

THE NEW TACTICS OF INFANTRY

IMPORTANT MILITARY WORKS.

THE NEW TACTICS OF

INFANTRY

(Studies in.)

By MAJOR W. VON SCHERFF.

TRANSLATED BY

COLONEL LUMLEY GRAHAM,
LATE 18TH (ROYAL IRISH) REGIMENT.

HENRY S. KING & Co.,
65, CORNHILL, & 12, PATERNOSTER ROW, LONDON.
1873.

TABLE OF CONTENTS.

—

PART I.

WAR TIME.

PART II.

THE PEACE SCHOOL.

SOME REMARKS BY THE TRANSLATOR.

— · —

AMONGST the many important subjects now under discussion in the military world, none is more important than, indeed, I believe I may safely say, none is so important as, the subject of the following studies.

By this time soldiers of all nations are agreed, almost without exception, that with the *new* arms *new* tactics are required. Some have long held this opinion and have been striving to spread it ever since the rifled musket came into general use. The introduction of rifled cannon and of breechloaders made the necessity for change more imperative and more obvious, so that at length almost everyone who reflects at all upon such matters has become a convert. The few who hold to the saying "*new* arms *old* tactics," are not likely to exercise much influence upon future war, and may safely be ignored.

But though we may all, in England as elsewhere, be convinced of the necessity for *new* tactics, there is plenty of reason for difference of opinion as to the

nature of this innovation which it is desirable to intro-
duce. And here it is that much study is required, and
that the opinions of practical men like Major von
Scherff who write under the fresh impression of the
best possible experience in such matters, that of the
battle-field, are extremely valuable, particularly to
men who, like most Englishmen of the present day,
are from the force of circumstances compelled to be
more theoretical than practical in such matters.

Now we all know that many things which appear
very good in theory turn out very badly in practice,
but why so? Simply because the theory had not a
practical foundation. The Prussian soldiers who first
used the needle-gun were, it may be said, mere theorists, but the theories were based upon practical considerations and careful study, so that they developed
themselves into most successful execution. Still
actual practice showed the Prussians that their
theories were at fault in many points, and they
have ever since been busy in profiting by the lessons
from which they feel that they have still much to
learn.

We English have now as fine an opportunity as
can fall to the lot of theorists, having had the advantage of watching some gigantic tactical experiments
carried out in a most exhaustive manner at the cost

of our neighbours, and receiving afterwards the benefit of their opinions upon the result.

Let us only study these opinions carefully upon their own merits, and neither adopt them with blind enthusiasm because they are " Prussian," or reject them with stolid prejudice because they are " Un-English," and "not suited to our national characteristics."

By the way, I have more than once heard it gravely asserted that fighting in skirmishing order is not " suited to our national characteristics." If I thought so, I should say the sooner we get a new suit of " characteristics " the better, but I don't think so, having read of our famous old " light division," and having seen what our men could do in the Kafir bush under Eyre. The reader will, I hope, pardon me for drawing his attention to one remarkable point of difference between " Studies on Tactics," written by soldiers who knew battle by practice like Major von Scherff, and those written by men who, like many of our later English essayists, only know it by theory, I mean the great stress which the former class lays upon the *moral* effect of a tactical formation, whilst the attention of the latter class is almost entirely confined to the *material* and *mechanical* side of the question. This is quite natural, for I believe those who have seen most of war attach the greatest importance to moral as distinguished from mere material considerations.

I cannot conclude these few introductory remarks more fitly than with the concluding sentence of Major von Scherff's studies :—

" May we be able to find time and opportunity for these lessons, lest war should have to teach us what we ought already to have learnt in peace, what like is battle ? "

L. G.

March, 1873.

STUDIES

ON THE

NEW TACTICS OF INFANTRY.

INTRODUCTION.

—•—

THE general adoption of the rifled musket, soon
followed by that of the rifled cannon, has impressed a
very different character upon the tactical literature of
all European armies, if we compare that of the last
fifteen years or so (that is to say, from the time of the
Crimean war), with that of the previous period ; and
the great wars which have been waged during these later
years have contributed powerfully to the same result ;—
for whilst the tactical writings of the period antecedent
to the date above mentioned were almost without exception mere text-books, calculated to set before the
reader and to make him practically acquainted with
the great principles of modern tactics as then determined (which was often done in a masterly manner) ;
on the other hand, the more recent works have been,

and are to the present day, mostly of a controversial nature, written, with more or less ability, but not always quite to the point, to discuss the changes in tactics apparently rendered necessary by the new fire-arms. Speaking generally, the debate has been narrowed to two questions :—

What general influence do the new arms exert upon the commander with reference to tactical operations; upon his selection of the offensive or defensive ?

How do they affect his manner of conducting either? (a question of elementary tactics, drill).

Now, although upon the former of these two questions opinions are pretty well reconciled, and nearly unanimous, the latter has not been settled definitively even by the last war between France and Germany, and we still see military men everywhere occupied with theoretical argument and practical experiment upon elementary tactics, especially with reference to infantry, seeking after a solution of the problem.

The necessity of finding such has been brought home to all more closely by the war of 1870—71, and has been accepted more readily than perhaps was the case before.

In that campaign the Prussian company-column triumphantly asserted its position as satisfying in the most complete manner hitherto discovered the altered requirements of tactics. Still it is just in the Prussian-German army itself that the conviction has gained ground most thoroughly ;

1. That what has hitherto been accomplished in this way is by no means absolutely exhaustive; that—

2. We owe the successful result of this formation mainly to our long familiarity with it in peace time: hence that—

3. Our present peaceful leisure—who knows how long it may last?—must be taken advantage of to provide our infantry tactics with a firm foundation based upon the experience gained in war; to establish a system more adapted to our present requirements than has been hitherto the case; so as to be able without prejudice to act on the field of battle as we have been accustomed to do on the drill-ground, and to be less dependent than we have hitherto been upon the personal inspiration of subordinate officers, however well justified this dependence may have been up to this time.

It is the school of peace—no one will now deny it—which provides an army with the cement necessary for enabling it to withstand the enormous friction of the battle-field. It is the established system to which the men have been long accustomed which gives to a standing army its immense superiority over the dilettantism of the mere levy.

Whatever system of battle-formations we adopt, the simpler, clearer, more unchangeable it is, so much the better for our requirements in every way; it will never check self-reliance or the exercise of individual skill, unless it is based on false principles, whilst where these qualities are at a low ebb—a case which may possibly arise—it will be a powerful aid in critical moments.

The present time seems to be in some measure favourable to the discovery of such a system, for the following reasons. As the possession of rifled guns and breechloaders will soon be common to all armies, the era of progress in the manufacture of firearms may, speaking generally, be considered closed for the immediate future. Although improvements may still be made constantly, we may yet consider ourselves for the present safe from such sudden surprises, from such startling and revolutionary novelties as were rifled guns and breechloaders when they first appeared.

Even repeating rifles and shrapnel shell contain at least no unexpected elements. On the other hand the *practical* experience of a great war, rich to excess in examples of battle, and in which both parties had the advantage of the most improved armament, gives to *theory* the so much needed aid. The following study is intended to contribute towards a work which is admitted to be both necessary and possible.

It does not pretend of itself to accomplish this work.

Based upon theoretical materials which may be considered as in every way exhaustive, and upon the practical examples of the last great wars, it will place the questions requiring decision impartially before the reader, not refraining at the same time from the expression of the writer's individual opinion or from criticism.

It will deal in turn, and as far as at present appears necessary, with the two main questions above alluded to.

CHAPTER I.

EVERY improvement in firearms produces a powerful impression that the *Defensive* has thereby gained an accession of strength. This feeling is all the more natural because a purely defensive attitude in the open field was first rendered possible by the invention of firearms and of gunpowder. In earlier days battles took the form of encounters in which both sides took the offensive, or else the defender was driven to make use of fortification to an extent far surpassing the practice of the present day.

Firearms and the Defensive are as much allied in our minds as are " l'arme blanche " and the Offensive ; in neither case can we well imagine the allies separated. " The better the firearm, the stronger the defence " is, therefore, a maxim the justice of which has always exerted its influence upon military operations since firearms have become general, and which has not yet quite lost its power.

So it was after the Crimean war, when the rifled musket, and so after the Bohemian campaign, when the breechloader, respectively made their *début* in the field. In each case theory raised its voice very loudly in favour of the principle of the *Defence*, and if the book-tacticians of those days had been worthy of credit, the war of 1870—71 should have bloomed into one of the finest specimens of a war of positions, in which, as is well known, the art of *beating* gives place to that of *not being beaten.*

This theory was deduced in a curious manner from our latest war-experience, each time in an indirect way, that is to say, the new arm was in both campaigns victorious in *Offence;* nevertheless we are told that it should properly give more power to the *Defence.* The fact that in 1859 the Austrian rifle did not hold its own against the smoothbore with which the French were still mostly armed, was accounted for by the action of the French rifled cannon. But, as was still maintained, "rifled guns and muskets must infallibly make the Defensive invincible."

It is a remarkable and interesting fact that at a time when these defensive theories had obtained pretty general approval, both in literature and even in other ways, the Austrians in 1866 would have nothing to say to them, and setting at naught the dictates of nature and tradition, rushed almost fanatically into the *Offensive*—to be everywhere beaten ; and that when the tables were turned and many voices were raised against that one-sided theory to reject it, the French in 1870 went upon the opposite tack, and, like the Austrians, acting contrary to their nature and traditions, servilely followed a *Defensive* system—to be in like manner everywhere beaten !

These striking contradictions show plainly enough that the formula of the " certain shot " is not infallible, when we have to decide upon the absolute merit of this or that tactical formation.

It must be confessed that the critics recovered themselves pretty soon from the first panic, so to say, which was created by the general introduction of rifled arms, and resting upon the experiences of 1859, they met the theory of the absolute *Defensive* with the argument that it was not so much the accuracy of the new arms as their low trajectory which rendered them such valuable allies to the Defence. With regard to breechloaders, it was asserted even before 1866 that their rapidity of fire would serve the assailant at least as well as it would the defender. In fact the more portable, moveable, handy, and quick-firing a gun is, so much the more suited is it to the attacking party, which is compelled to be constantly in movement, a condition unfavourable to the use of firearms. The development of artillery from the gun of position to its present degree of perfection was a consequence of this conviction, just as the rapid-firing infantry of Frederick the Great, acting as it did on the offensive, was an example of its justice.

Thus a very decided opposition to the defensive hobby grew out of purely technical considerations. Is it necessary to enlarge upon the decisive question of *morale?*

We think not, after 1870, after 1866, after the whole of Prussia's history. Indeed it may appear superfluous to moot the question at all at the present day, and in our country! The theory of the superiority of the *Offensive* is for the time being so firmly rooted that a reaction is not much to be feared.

And yet even with us the time of the doubters has not long passed away; a single instance of failure on the part of the *Offensive*—always a possible event—would again wake up these theorists, who, in accordance with their critical German nature, would once more produce their coldly reasoned "*demonstrations founded upon the nature of the arm.*"

After all we might remain indifferent to this if the question raised in tactical literature, "*Defensive or Offensive?*" had not led to another tactical inquiry, which in its bearing on the principles of the training of our infantry is, perhaps, no less important than the former one.

The well-known school-definitions describe "victory" as the end aimed at in every "conflict;" moreover, they pronounce the "*Offensive*" to be almost without exception the only "road to victory;" whilst they proclaim the "*Defensive*" to be a "negation of victory," which to become decisively victorious must needs "change its nature" and become *Offensive.* We thus come to the following conclusion:

" That to obtain a decisive victory we must adopt
the *Offensive* from the first, or else take to it after a
Defence successfully conducted."

Though these maxims are only of primary and absolute importance to the strategical side of the discussion,
yet they doubtless have the value of a principle also
from the tactical point of view. A victory gained
simply by acting tactically on the defensive, without
any offensive return or pursuit, and merely compelling
the enemy to retreat, will never decide a campaign,
but will, at the most, prepare the way for this result.

But in every battle it should be our aim at once to
attain the decisive result, which consists in the tactical
annihilation of the enemy.

When, therefore, we come to treat of tactical formations, we shall necessarily resume the discussion as to
the fundamental conditions, and as to the chances of
these two only possible methods of attaining victory.

But we find in war, besides the decisive battles
alluded to, a great number of engagements, that is to
say, of opportunities for fighting, in which certainly one
side, and perhaps the other also, does not attempt to
attain to any decisive result ; in other words, to gain a
victory in the sense of a definitive overthrow of the
enemy ; where the possession of a certain point or
portion of a position, or the gain of a certain amount
of time, is of more importance to you than is the
actual loss of men at the same time caused to the
enemy.

Such engagements must always naturally assume an offensive or defensive character, but never represent the *Offensive* or *Defensive* in the sense of seeking to obtain victory by the adoption of either principle. Hence it ensues that the way in which troops are handled will differ according to which of the two objects you have in view, and thus, that the formations which suit the one case will not be entirely adapted to the other.

In order then to promote a clear system of instruction in time of peace, the end we are now aiming at, it appears necessary, both in theory and practice, to establish the distinction between the *fighting which aims at a decisive result, and that which aims at no decisive result (to which we will apply the term " Temporising combat ")*, more clearly than has been done heretofore.

Then in treating of *fighting which aims at a decisive result*, the further question crops up of *Offensive or Defensive ?* and we shall have occasion again to inculcate, both theoretically and practically, that there should be no such thing as a *Defensive* without a development of the *Offensive* from it.

This study, then, would give the foundation upon which the details of a sound modern system of infantry tactics may be based, a foundation which, assuming the form of a " Battle-guide," would establish principles somewhat such as follow :

1. Every officer with an independent command

finding himself in front of the enemy has at once to make up his mind as to the following points :— whether he can or should, cannot or should not, aim at a decisive result; this will depend upon whether he is strong enough, upon the general situation, whether other troops are engaged before him, what there is behind him, and so forth ; or whether his situation is likely to be improved by a temporising combat or not. This would be undertaken to give time for reinforcements to arrive, for the purpose of misleading the enemy, or for gaining better information ;

2. Should he feel bound to answer both questions in the negative, he should do his utmost to avoid or break off all engagements;

3. If he thinks himself justified in entering into a decisive action, he should adopt the principle of the *Offensive;* should he, without being momentarily strong enough for such a course, be able to reckon upon receiving sufficient reinforcements, he should carry on a *temporising combat* in such a manner that, as far as possible, the enemy may be deprived of the initiative in assuming the *Offensive,* whilst threatened with it at the same time by him (see the chapter on the *temporising combat*).

4. Only under very peculiar and exceptional circumstances, or when the nature of the ground peremptorily demands it, should he accept battle from the first in a defensive position.

We will now proceed to consider the three chief forms of tactical action, which result from the foregoing considerations : the *Offensive*, the *Defensive-Offensive*, and the *Temporising Combat*.

CHAPTER II.

THE OFFENSIVE.

THE outward evidence of victory, hence the object we strive for, is the forcible expulsion of the enemy from that spot on which he wishes to maintain himself. All action of troops in battle consists in the employment of the power either of dealing blows or of withstanding them. Both taken together constitute the fighting capacity of a body of troops, that quality without which the troops as a body cannot exist, and the loss of which entails their destruction as such. This power, then, of giving blows and of withstanding them—in other words, the attacking power and the resisting power, encounter one another in every action, with a view to mutual destruction ; victory inclines to the side gifted with the greatest fighting capacity. In order to be victorious, it is therefore necessary to be stronger than your adversary at a given time and place.

This greater degree of strength is obtained either by the physical and numerical, or by the moral superiority of one force over the other ; if possible, by all combined.

The sum total of these advantages represents the attacking power of the force on the offensive, and, in like manner, the resisting power of that on the defensive. Now, in order that a force on the offensive may be able to develop with effect its maximum of attacking power, and make use of it to the utmost, it should adopt a formation favourable, as far as possible, to the following requirements :—

To the *very greatest mobility;* for the possibility of a successful *Offensive* is, above all, dependent on forward movement ; further,

To the *greatest possible security from the effects of the enemy's fire;* that most dangerous foe to the *Offensive,* because it damages most intensely the assailant's attacking power, both physical and moral, and may cause him to hesitate, retire, give way before reaching the decisive point :

Lastly, to the greatest possible development of its own fire, at any rate, at the moment of actual collision, and, if possible, at an earlier stage of the combat also ; for the superiority of the assailant in this respect is absolutely necessary to give his attack the amount of power requisite to ensure a real *victory.*

The old system of tactics met these requirements by providing *formations in mass;* either in line or column.

The revolutionary wars introduced the *extended order*—the swarm of skirmishers.

The massive formations as developed by the Napoleonic wars, and as maintained down to the latest war-era, fulfilled more or less well all the above-mentioned general requirements for every offensive formation, or fulfilled, some more, others less well, *as measured by the armament of those days.*

Formation in extended order, in other words the action of individuals, seems at that period to have been a mere accessory, rendered necessary, to speak generally, rather by the altered method of conducting military operations (taking advantage of ground), than by the nature of the arms.

The attempts made from time to time to raise this extended order to the first rank failed during the revolutionary period, owing to the inefficiency of those who undertook the enterprise; and these attempts were not renewed, because they were as yet not necessary; nevertheless, the combat of Saalfeld may be cited as an example of an action in which victory was gained entirely by the use of extended order offensively.

Since the first steps were taken in the manufacture of the new arms, this formation has forced its way more and more into the foreground; in 1859, the rifle placed it upon an equality with the old formation; in 1870-71, the breechloader established its superiority over it.

The following fact is finally established in opposition to all previous theories, that in the war of 1870-71, the enemy's position (whether in the open field or on the borders of woods and villages), *was invariably carried by swarms of skirmishers,* followed only at greater or less distance by lines and columns in close order.

We may therefore affirm, that *individual order has actually become the only battle-formation for infantry.*

We place the expression *individual order* in contrast to *order in mass,* and understand by the latter term, a formation in which each individual soldier has his assigned place, which he must not leave ; by the former, a formation in which each soldier has likewise a place assigned to him, but in a general way, and with the power of changing it at pleasure within certain fixed limits.

We substitute the expressions "order in mass" and "individual order" for those in general use, namely, "close order" and "extended" or "dissolved" (aufge-löst) order,—first, because the formation of skirmishers, which is implied by both the latter terms, may often take very close order; and, secondly, because the actual dissolution of order is never recognised.[*]

These are but words : of little consequence in argument, when the disputants understand one another's meaning, but in practice not altogether void of meaning and valueless. We hardly require

[*] Henceforth in the translation, I shall take the liberty of making use of the expressions "close order" and "extended order," because more convenient and more familiar to English ears than the literal translation of "massenordnung" and "einzelordnung."—(Tr.)

any further arguments to prove that extended order
is more adapted to the three above-named main
requirements for offensive action than any formation
in close order.

Moreover, we may safely allege, that no considerations of that kind weighed against the general and
much earlier adoption of extended order for infantry
attack. The actual objection lay rather in the instinc-
tive, though it might be unexpressed, conviction, that
with the means of training troops then available, it
would be impossible with skirmishers to obtain the
amount of *attacking-power* indispensable to offensive
action.

In the first place, it was thought seriously that it
would not be possible to provide a sufficient number of
skirmishers ; and, secondly, no great reliance was
placed on the *moral* force of extended order. This
arose from the traditions of the period, and tradition
hinders men oftener than we think from finding
Columbus' egg.

The promotion of *extended order* to the rank of a
tactical formation only became possible when value
began to be attached to the development of the
soldier's faculties by instruction, and on the other
hand, this only took place when the improvement of
firearms began to make the *extended order* more and
more necessary.|

Thus, as is generally the case in this world, supply
met demand, one having produced the other, until we

reached the present stage, when we have to perfect the means which have supplied the demand.

The controversial literature of later years, and war-experience, have supplied such inexhaustible materials for showing how this may be accomplished that it would be difficult to say anything new upon the subject; we only require these materials to be arranged methodically. This arrangement must evidently be in keeping with those general principles applicable to the *Offensive*, which have held good in all ages.

We must now, before proceeding further, revert briefly to these principles, although, in doing so, we shall go over long-familiar ground.

Every attack has to go through three stages :—

The period of preparation,

The moment of accomplishment, and of the greatest strain on the faculties, and

The period of reaction and of recovery.

It is sufficient to indicate these stages; we are not here called upon to prove their " raison d'être."

Let us only premise, in order to avoid misunderstanding, that by the expression "preparation of the attack," * we by no means understand the same thing as the " opening of the fight." †

The "opening of the fight" implies the several acts of reconnoitring the enemy and the ground, of gaining time for deployment, of coming to a determina-

* Vorbereitung des Angriffs.
† Einleitung des Gefechts.

tion upon the object to be fought for, and upon the means to be employed ; that is to say, of making your dispositions and giving out your orders ; all of which belongs, according to our previous classification, to the domain of the "*Temporising combat.*"

In the observations which follow, we will look upon this period as passed by, and will treat of the " preparation " simply as the first step of an attack, the direction of which, and the means to be employed in making which, have already been quite settled.

If in any matter connected with war we may consider thorough energy of will as the most necessary condition of success, this will apply most certainly to the *attack*, in which our warlike energy is most completely drawn upon.

This being then admitted, we must actually take into consideration whatever relates to the theory of the attack, and to its practical execution.

This will be the place to treat more particularly of those elements which produce energy of action.

First of all comes *clearness of judgment*—clearness in two ways—both with regard to the *end* to be attained and to the *means* to be employed.

This might appear to some so self-evident as not to deserve particular mention, and yet whoever studies military history with care will find how much powder has been wasted, how much human blood has been uselessly spilt, from want of this clearness.

The critic cannot fail to observe that a large propor·

tion of the actions in every war, both ancient and modern, have been commenced without consideration, carried on without energy, and brought to a close without advantage, by one or both parties.

We are not now speaking of *temporising* combats, or of those undertaken for reconnoitring purposes; these have an actual object, and a real use; we refer to that scuffling sort of fight in which some commanders think themselves bound to engage every time that they see an enemy, and which is often commenced by a go-a-head advanced-guard before its leader has calculated what he wishes to gain, or can gain by it; before he has asked himself the question, whether it may not, on the whole, be prejudicial to the general operations. Once commenced, the fight must be carried on by the troops which successively come up, because in military affairs most especially the saying comes true, that he who says A must also say B. It is only lucky when a "skrimmage," of this kind, at least, ends without any decided result, or when he who commenced it without knowing why, finds as the affair goes on, means and energy enough to bring it to a decisive conclusion.

But still, this sort of thing does no good. Therefore in the chapter on the *Offensive and Defensive,* it is recommended that a commander should avoid all fights which do not offer any positive and attainable objective. Therefore, again, we consider it of primary importance that whoever determines upon

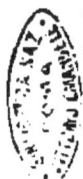

the *Offensive should undertake it with his whole energy,
and should make full use of all the means at his disposal.*

This also may seem self-evident; and yet how many
attacks one sees made with half or a quarter of the
force available, under the influence of that barrack-
square theory, false as it is, of the possibility of renewing the attack with the second line, and of that equally
false school-theory of the necessity of holding back the
reserves.

This is the moment to devote a few words to the
importance of the *introductory* (as distinguished from
the *preparatory*) period of the attack, of the form and
conduct of which we shall treat in the chapter on the
temporising combat.

The enormous effect of artillery and infantry fire
more than ever impels masses of troops which
come under it to bring things to as rapid a conclusion as possible : more than ever, therefore, is the
habit of quick decision necessary to the leader, and
more than ever should the masses be kept back until
the plan of action is determined, for which the *introductory* period is alone available, the possibility of a
subsequent change of plan being, moreover, much
more restricted than formerly.

As soon as the leader has determined upon his
mode of action, he has, so to say, cast the dice, and
victory depends upon the throw.

From that moment, no hesitation, no half measures,

are allowable. The commander's judgment as to "where" and " when " will unalterably and irrevocably determine the result of the operation.

This is the work of the *introductory* stage, and this it is which makes that stage decisive to the leader of an attack. The determination has been taken. Now to the conditions of execution.

We have already shown that to have a numerical and moral superiority over the enemy at a specified time and place is a main condition of success : to this must be added, as elements of victory, mobility, certainty, and a formation calculated to get full value from the arms.

Your attack must have its fixed objective; it must be conducted as directly as possible, and without a check; it must be executed with the whole of the force at your disposal.

These three principles, as universal experience shows us, are the necessary foundation of all attack.

With all disposable force! You can never be too strong when making an attack, for you never can be perfectly sure of what forces you may encounter, or at what moment the defender may make a counter attack, which will only be omitted by an apathetic foe. But the repulse of every attack exercises a demoralising influence on the assailant, and the possibility of renewing the assault with fresh troops, which can alone justify the non-employment in the first instance of your whole available force, will always be diminished by a first unsuccessful attempt. Whether the attack prove successful or not, it is better that all your forces should be concentrated, as both the physical effect upon the enemy and the moral stimulus upon yourself will be thereby augmented, and danger will be diminished, both directly and indirectly, if the masses are held together under the influence of one chief.

Infantry being able to maintain a standing fight is not, like cavalry, put "hors combat" by a repulse, and the stronger the force the more true this is. Hence the reserve which infantry proceeding to the attack leaves behind it should be reduced to a minimum, being only intended to cover its rear in case of need, perhaps to hold a defile which may happen to be in dangerous proximity; it will be best if this reserve for the infantry is furnished by the other arms.

An attack made with only a part of your force at once awakens the idea of the possibility of non-success.

Now a commander should weigh in his own mind all the chances of defeat, and seek beforehand to provide against them; but if once soldiers engaged in an assault have the idea of retreat in their heads they are already half beaten.

It is possible for the attack to fail, but it is impossible for us to go back. The sword cuts or flies to pieces, the army conquers, or there will only be its fragments to collect.

To make an *attack* in such a spirit as this, you

require your whole available strength; otherwise it ceases to be an *attack*, and becomes merely a *tentative advance with a retreat quickly impending.*

As directly as possible, and without a check! It naturally must deaden the energy of your attack and diminish your chance of success if you take a round-about way to reach your object. Quickness of execution is one of the chief elements of success, and is most seriously impaired by any deviation from the straight direction of the onset. However great the advantage of directing your attack upon the flank of an enemy, it is nevertheless imperative that the measures for doing this should be taken when they can be carried out unseen and unmolested by fire; as, for instance, during the *introductory* period; and such a manœuvre will never be favourable to success if attempted by an oblique movement under fire, or by a change of front (which takes up a long time, and is therefore prejudicial), after you are already engaged. The destructive effect of the enemy's projectiles will produce confusion as the inevitable consequence of such a complicated attempt; this will be followed by hesitation and a full stop; the attentive foe will take advantage of such a dangerous movement for making a doubly damaging counter stroke.

Straight to the front—forward is the word of command suited to the attack, and the only command which is sure of its moral impulse upon the soldier.

The fixed objective! Only the *first* point to be reached should be given as the object of attack. Nothing can be more prejudicial than to make a determination as to a second objective before the first is attained. The previous indication of what is to happen *if* the first point is carried is as premature as the simultaneous direction of the attacking force on objects which are not in the same line.

No attack should have more than one objective at a time ; whatever follows will require further orders.

It is the duty of the supreme command to confine operations to the end in view, and it is the duty of the operating force to keep strictly within the limits assigned. An offensive action to be carried out with *calculated energy* (to which mere "*élan*" is in strong contrast), should advance by spurts from one mark aimed at to another. We must make allowance for the moment of reaction, the natural consequence of every attack, and of the extreme tension of the nerves, which is its inevitable accompaniment. Before this moment of weakness has passed away, a leader with clear and sure views will not proceed to the solution of further problems.

On the other hand, a force which ignores these natural pauses in the conflict, and which oversteps those lines of demarcation between its stages in a fragmentary way will not be as reliable for manœuvre— as much in hand—as could be wished. That blind forward rush beyond a position which has been carried, that reckless charge upon the enemy, without a thought of your neighbours, has gathered many a laurel, but has also compromised many a success, and has led to many a repulse : it has only cost the perpetrators their lives, but it has cost the army victory.

Therefore, *only one object at a time!* So much for the general subject. Let us now turn to the special formations for the three stages of the attack.

I. THE PREPARATORY STAGE.

The necessity of preparing the way for an attack by the fire of artillery and skirmishers has already been inculcated in former lessons on warfare. We shall therefore have less to deal with the general question than with the strength of troops intended for this purpose, and with the mode of handling them. The old principle of extending only as few skirmishers as possible, of letting "out of hand" only as many as are absolutely necessary for the end in view, however well suited to the epoch such a maxim may have been, has suffered considerable modification from the improvement in firearms.

There is no doubt that the accession of strength which has accrued to the *Defence* from improved fire-arms has produced its first result in the increased necessity for *preparatory action*, and, consequent upon this, in the augmentation of the force employed for this purpose.

The rule which formerly was considered so important, of only reinforcing a line of skirmishers little by little, soon proved itself in practice to be more dangerous and more productive of loss than the extension of a sufficient number from the very first, that is to say, from the time of coming within the zone of rifle fire. After substituting the latter rule for the old one, we must next determine what is a sufficient number.

In view of the increased powers of resistance of the Defence, the answer must certainly be, *as many rifles as from the nature of the ground can be brought effectively into play.*

If the preparation of an attack is really to be effectual, in other words, if it is to shake the defender physically and morally, it is of primary importance that the same should be continued without interruption from the very commencement to the moment of actual impact. If the last rush only takes place some time after the preparatory fire has been interrupted, although this may possibly have materially weakened the defenders, there will be no question of seriously shaking their morale, always supposing them to be good troops. On the contrary, the fact of the artillery fire having been really or apparently silenced, will have exalted their courage.

Now, as the fire of every skirmisher armed with a breechloader may be looked upon as uninterrupted, and as each individual requires for the full use of his arm, when in movement, about one-and-a-half

paces in width, we may reckon the greatest possible
strength desirable for troops engaged in the *preparatory* operation at *one man to every one-and-
a-half paces of the front of attack.* This calculation
will, then, without considering the question of loss
which we shall deal with hereafter, represent the
maximum strength of skirmishers told off for the
preparation. As at this moment we have only to
consider the amount of fire to be developed, we must
look upon every man placed in the line of skirmishers
who cannot contribute to this, owing to want of space,
as hurtful to the general effect, inasmuch as he is unnecessarily increasing the materials for loss.

Given, therefore, a body of troops of a specified
strength, it will be at once necessary to determine how
broad can, should, or must be its front of attack.

In order to do this, we must examine another phase
of the requirements to be demanded from the fire
which prepares the way for attack.

We have already noticed the necessity for an uninterrupted fire from the very commencement of the
action up to the moment of actual collision. And to
be more precise, it is necessary to remark, that we
time this commencement from the moment at which
the advanced troops, whose mission consists in preparing the way for the attack by attempting to shake
the enemy's powers of resistance, have reached (we
will explain later how) the point from which their fire
will be most effective. It is not at present necessary

for us to explain our reasons for choosing this moment.
In the present condition of firearms this point would
be between 400 and 200 paces from the spot at which
we propose to force the enemy's position.

Now it is not in human nature for even the best
troops in the world to hold out for more than a few
minutes whilst they and their opponents are keeping
up a rapid independent fire, such as it would be, upon
one another at so close and effective a range (for we
presume both parties to be equally well armed). Not
to mention the actual loss, which is often not at all in
proportion to the expenditure of ammunition, the moral
effect of such a fire upon the nerves is such that the
crisis will be hurried on very quickly by the excitement thus produced.

We must not imagine the defender with the advantage, which he has, of the more favourable position, to
be in other respects inferior to the assailant; we must
not suppose him to bolt; therefore, after a very short
time, the attacking force will either be seized with the
impulse to rush forward to close quarters, or to turn
tail. Hence, it is advisable, in order to meet either
the one case or the other, for the main body destined
to give the actual shock to be up in line with the
advanced skirmishers (who are not of themselves
strong enough to do the work) by this time, or better
still, a little sooner.

On the other hand, it is naturally the interest of the
main body not to come up with the advanced skir-

mishers, that is to say, into the zone of serious loss, before their fire has been doing its work for some time; if possible indeed, not until the probable moment of the crisis.

Until then, it should endeavour to keep as far as practicable out of the effectual range of the enemy's fire, and by reconciling as far as possible these contradictory requirements, nay, necessities, we obtain the distance which should intervene between the main body and the advanced line which is preparing the way for it.

Assuming, from the lessons of the late war, that a rapid independent fire from both sides, such as above supposed, cannot well last above five minutes without bringing things to a crisis, we may fix the distance of the main body from the advanced troops, when this critical period commences, at not exceeding 500 paces.

On perfectly open ground, the main body will not be able to get nearer until the decisive moment when the commencement of the rapid fire in front will force it to push on. But even if it should follow the first line of skirmishers at no more than about 300 paces distance, it will still be necessary to interpose an intermediate body between the two, keeping in mind that the said skirmishers are in single rank with intervals of from one to one-and-a-half paces.

The advance of this line to within effective range will naturally be attended with loss, and probably very

serious loss, the materials for repairing which immediately it is necessary to have close at hand, if
you wish the preparation for the attack to be uninterrupted.

This *support* must be stronger, or may be weaker,
according to the degree of cover afforded by the
ground as you approach the enemy.   It may be considered as a maxim approved by practice, and generally
received in theory, that the support should be at least
half as strong as the line of skirmishers, and range
between that strength and one equal to theirs.

But in order to give the necessary impetus to the
attack, it will be undoubtedly advisable that our main
body should at least equal in strength the total of the
two front lines, both of which are actually only intended
to prepare the way.

This question of what is requisite for each separate
stage of the attack has led us back by a roundabout
way to our starting-point, namely, what should be the
extent of front for an attacking force of specified
strength ?

This *normal extent of front* may be estimated from
the following premises : that an attacking force will
devote from one-half to two-thirds of its total strength
to the *main body*, from one-half to one-third of that
strength to the *advance*, and that from one-half to two-
thirds of the latter force will be extended at intervals
of from one to one-and-a-half paces.   In other words,
and with due consideration for attendant circum-

stances: *the normal front of attack of a battalion on open ground should not exceed 300 paces.**

It remains now to be mentioned, that in making this calculation, we have as yet entirely left out of count the third stage of the attack. We must return to it presently.

Further, it appears from what has come out on our way to this result, that the normal front of attack of a specified force increases in proportion to the amount of cover afforded by the ground which it has to traverse. In other words, the more cover there is, the closer can the main body keep to the advance, whilst the losses of the latter will be at the same time smaller; the more both these conditions are realised, the more superfluous will be, or at least the less strong need be, the intervening supports; what we spare in this way we can employ eventually for strengthening the *advance* which should in principle be as strong as possible; but as every rifle in the *advance* should be in action, this accession of strength will produce an extension *of front.*

This brings us, then, to the influence of the ground on the attack, and at the same time, to another branch of the inquiry, bearing, as above remarked, upon the preparatory stage; we mean, *the form in which the troops should be led on.*

---

* 200 rifles for the advanced line of skirmishers, 200 for the support, 400 for the main body; officers, supernumeraries, and casuals will make up the rest of the effective strength.

This consideration will also naturally lead us to determine the extreme limit of the offensive front of an attacking force. If, in discussing this subject, we assume the most trying conditions to be in force, namely, that the ground is open, the question of how to handle a line of skirmishers (and of this only we have here to treat) will be also solved for the more favourable conditions of more or less broken ground. Let us fix the point to be attained, namely, that from which rapid independent fire should be opened, at 300 paces from the enemy's main position.

Three different methods have been proposed in theory, and tried in practice, of bringing up a line of skirmishers to this point under heavy fire.

1. The advance of the *whole line in one body* with or without firing ;

2. The advance of the *whole line by a succession of rushes*, between which the men lie down and fire by word of command ;

3. The advance of the line by fractions, those on the move being covered by the fire of those halted.

All three methods demand, as an absolute necessity, the greatest possible expedition ; thus, as far as applicable, the use of running; also, the practice of lying down at every forced or voluntary halt. Being universally recognised, these points require here no further discussion. The rapid advance without a halt and without firing, must, undoubtedly, be acknowledged to be the most effective course, as long as it seems possible. But it can

only be followed to a certain extent, rather owing to
reasons founded upon the inner nature of man than,
perhaps, upon the force of outward circumstances ; and
let us not be misled by some exceptions under peculiarly favourable conditions. After having attained to
that distance from the enemy where a line of skirmishers begins to experience loss, particularly from
infantry fire, which cannot be put down simply to
chance shots, from that moment advance in the mode
referred to becomes difficult, slackens, finally comes to
a standstill.

One mode of overcoming the first stage of this
difficulty will be to open fire yourself. It will, in all
probability, have no effect worth mentioning upon your
adversary, still it will to a certain extent animate your
own people, as it will convey to them the impression that
they are no longer, as it were, opposed unarmed to the
enemy.   The danger of this course consists in the
probability of the fire, commenced at first sparingly
by individuals, becoming general, and thereby slacken-
ing the advance, which is to be avoided, as progress is
apt to become slower and slower, till at last you come
to a halt, the attitude best suited to the use of firearms.

To act in a really practical manner we are here more
than ever called upon to study human nature. A theory
which is only based upon "that can, that should, that
must not be," runs the risk of much too bitter checks,
when put in practice, for us to prefer laying too little
rather than too much stress upon the moral side of

the question (the effect on the spirit of the soldier), in our peace-habits. This reflection should induce us, in our peace exercises, to do what is perhaps the best in principle, in all cases to make allowance for human weakness as far as would actually be necessary.

For this reason we should be inclined to make it a fixed rule that the advance be made entirely *without firing* under artillery fire, and till within the outer space of infantry fire. In other words, the body of troops which is intended to prepare the way should extend on reaching the zone of artillery fire directed upon it (whether at once entirely or only by degrees is immaterial, but at all events the part destined to act as support should extend before it becomes a target even for artillery fire); the skirmishers should then advance as rapidly as possible without firing until they come under the infantry fire directed against them.

The advanced body should get over the ground from its first entry into action up to within 1000 *or* 800 *paces, if possible within* 600 *paces of the enemy, in one line.* We have here purposely made no mention of firing. It will be better to do without it, if possible, but if not, no harm will be done, as long as it is well regulated by command, and does not become too wild.

From this point onwards where the losses from the enemy's infantry cease to be accidental, and where we can make out our opponents clearly, or at any rate their position, being at the same time plainly visible to

them, it will in most cases be advisable to adopt one or
other form of *gradual* advance. Each of the two
above indicated methods offers undeniable advantages; that of *successive rushes in one body* gives
greater promise of maintaining order; whilst the *fractional* plan gives greater security. If, on our own part,
we speak out decisively in favour of the latter method,
we do not found our opinion so much upon the more
or less cogent reasons which theorists have up to this
time adduced (for instance, the advance being covered
by fire), as upon the following considerations :—

We have hitherto been supposing the case of an
attack, conducted by a comparatively small body, but
if we now imagine instead a similar operation, but executed by a force of several battalions side by side, and
all having the same objective, it is evident that the
long line of skirmishers necessary to prepare the way
for such an attack cannot possibly be directed by one
leader either by voice or bugle amidst the tumult and
the din of battle. But in addition to this evident
difficulty, there are other causes which, in the case of
long lines, lead to a fractional advance. The resistance
will not always be equally vigorous along the whole
front; the fire brought to bear by the defender against
the assailant during the different stages of his advance
will be weakened perhaps, sometimes at one place,
sometimes at another, often only for a few moments; a
lucky shell, or the fortunate exposure of a part of the
enemy's line of defence, if quickly taken advantage of,

may favour the onset at particular points ; whilst at the
same moment the difficulties of the attack are doubled
on other parts of the front ; even a plain, to all appearance as open as possible, will offer here and there little
accidents of ground favourable to the assailant, which
he will take advantage of, if intelligent ; and so forth.
Thus, in the case of a long line, a *fractional* advance
becomes the most natural course, and is adopted at once
instinctively, and because the impulse to action felt at
one point cannot be very quickly communicated along
the whole line.   But what must inevitably and without
doubt occur in the case supposed will very often be
found the best course, and even necessary, with shorter
lines.   Even with a front of a few hundred paces, when
a whole line is advancing in one body, alternately rushing on and lying down by word of command, it will
sometimes happen that, even in the most apparently
open ground, some group or other of skirmishers will
find its fire most unexpectedly masked by an undula-
tion which had not been before remarked.   The course
then which must imperatively be followed whenever
the front is very extensive had better be adopted as
the general rule under all circumstances.

There are, however, two arguments which may be
adduced in favour of the system of *successive rushes in one
body* as against that of the *fractional advance.* In the first
place, it is urged that the moral impulse to go forward
will be more easily maintained if all jump up and run
on together ; that the difficulty, which is well recog-

nised, of inducing skirmishers to leave cover, however slight, will be more easily overcome if the officers of the whole line set the example, enforcing it at the same time with voice and signal (whistle). Again, a *fractional* advance, particularly if the fractions are small, will very likely lead to sections getting in front of one another, the fire of those behind, on which, however, one has to count, thus being masked by those in front, and the whole line being thus easily thrown into disorder.

These arguments are not without force, but they do not appear sufficiently conclusive to warrant the adoption of the system which they support as one of universal application (one fixed by regulation), because in practice the exceptions will be numerous. It would appear to be more advisable to strive to remedy the disadvantages of the *fractional* system by advancing only in entire divisions (züge *)—(thus gaining the moral influence of the officers)—and not more than from fifty to eighty paces at a time beyond the adjacent fraction which is halted ; moreover, by practising this manœuvre so constantly at drill as to make it into a second nature.

However much one may be tempted—for the sake of order—to make strict regulations as to the succession, for instance, in which the separate divisions are to move forward, it will be well to guard against this

---

* Three of which form a company when drawn up, as for action, two deep.—(Tr.)

temptation, as it will lead to artificial refinements impossible of execution under fire. It will be found advisable in peace to allow the leader of the line of skirmishers and his subordinates that liberty of action which would in war result from their appreciation of their own fire and of that of the enemy. The utmost we should do in this way is to fix a limit of time, at drill, for each section to remain halted (it might be whilst two or three rounds are fired). On service this matter would settle itself.

This brings us to another question affecting the mode in which a *preparatory* force should be handled—namely, that of *command.*

It is a military principle, which we are hardly re quired to defend in this place, that a movement directed on one object should be under one head.

In order to act up to the spirit of this principle, it is necessary that wherever a body of troops is employed to gain some one object, which body is not a separate unit, but is composed of different sections independent of one another, it is necessary, we say, to assign to each section-commander a share of the work to be done as his special object.

In spite of all theorising upon the idea of the *tactical unit,* the most fanatical admirer of the company-column must confess that the company is too small a body to carry out an attack through all its three stages, always supposing the operation to be on a large scale.

Twelve company-columns will not be able to carry

out, each independently for itself, the preparation and execution of an attack, not to mention its third stage ; whilst *three* battalions are quite competent to do it.*

What is generally true of the companies is also applicable, only in a modified form, to separate battalions.

Three battalions, each acting independently, will be able to get well through the first two stages of an attack, but it will be hardly equal to the third stage.

We shall return to this subject in dealing with the further stages of the battle ; we only touched upon it in this place in order to arrive at the conclusion (a certain one, we think), that when it appears necessary, as above pointed out, to subdivide the object of attack into separate objectives, it will be well not to assign one of these to a smaller body than a battalion.

But, as we have already pointed out, the front of attack suited to a battalion may be estimated at about 300 paces, from which it appears evident that it would hardly do to assign to several battalions formed side by side the same special object of attack, such as a house, the entrance to a village, the corner of a wood, or such like.

We shall return to this subject likewise when we treat of the *execution* of the attack ; for the present it will suffice that it should be generally allowed that in practice each battalion on the front of attack should and will have its own special point to carry.

---

* It may be as well to remind the reader that a German battalion equals four companies.—(Tr.)

This being allowed, we must next inquire whether it is better for the battalion to have the two lines recognised as necessary for the *preparatory stage*, namely, skirmishers and supports, under one command as respects front or depth.

To be in accordance with the principle of one head for one task, we will at once dismiss the case, as not seriously debateable, of the possibility of all the companies of a battalion sharing about equally in the formation of the *advance* and of the *main body:* we have only, then, to consider whether two companies ranged side by side should from the first form both skirmishers and supports, or whether these companies should be drawn up one behind the other, one acting as skirmishers, the other as support.

To solve this question, it will be necessary to examine a little more closely the task which each line has to perform, and how their action is combined. The first, or skirmishing line has, in the supposed case of a battalion with an assigned object of attack, most undoubtedly a task complete in itself, and with one object in view.   This task consists in endeavouring to overwhelm with its fire from a front, not originally exceeding 300 paces, some always smaller portion of the enemy's position which has been pointed out, and thus to shake the defenders before the onslaught of the main body.

The point which the latter is to force should be first quite clearly made out, the most favourable spot being

chosen, after you have approached pretty close to
the enemy's position. Upon this point the fire will
then be concentrated as much as possible, which,
with a front of only 300 paces, may, with our present arms, proceed from the whole line, even if the
selected point chance to be opposite one flank.

It is evident that all this may be attained most
successfully by unity of command, and that, on the
other hand, considerations of space by no means render this unity impossible. The advantages of this unity
of command have, indeed, misled French tacticians
into wishing to break up a whole battalion into
skirmishers, when the attacking force consists of several
battalions. This is carrying it too far, and the arrangement must break down, because no one separate
objective can be assigned to such a line. Let us
now compare the case of a skirmishing line composed
of one company with that of one made up of two
halves of different companies (of course we suppose the
number of skirmishers in both cases to be equal). In
the latter case, we see the line led by two independent
commanders of equal powers, in close proximity to one
another. This must, of necessity, produce greater
difficulties in the way of command than when, as in
the former case, the skirmishers are all under one
leader. When it comes to advancing by successive
fractions, the full value will not be got out of the two
half companies as it will out of the one company accustomed to the signs and signals of its officers. More-

over, the opinions of the two commanders as to the moment at which it is advisable to extend the full number of skirmishers, or as to when it is necessary to ask for further reinforcements from the supports, will agree no better than will their views as to the time when the line should, according to the existing state of affairs, commence the rapid independent fire, which must be continued to the very moment of the final rush.

As we must understand the effective range for this fire to extend from 200 to nearly 400 paces, it is evident that the line of skirmishers runs the risk of partial checks from the different appreciation of the proper distance from which to commence rapid firing, which may be formed by the two officers, each of whom will only direct his attention to the other, so far as to avoid being left behind by him. Now these partial checks are the worst things that can happen in the preparatory stage.

Besides, it by no means follows that the two leaders will agree as to the best point for forcing the enemy's line ; hence, there will not be the concentration of fire which is so requisite for the success of the whole enterprise, for we should prefer the less well-chosen point of attack which has been well fired upon to one better selected but less well fired upon.

Again ; whilst a skirmishing line composed of one entire company gravitates naturally to its centre, because the one chief will, and must, have influence enough over his lieutenants to control their perhaps conflicting aims, it is not a mere matter of fancy to affirm that two separate companies moving side by side will have a decidedly centrifugal tendency, and (for we must always make allowance for human nature) will be sure to act accordingly in reality, in spite of all theory.

It will not be a sufficient answer to reply that the battalion commander will be on the spot to remedy all these drawbacks arising from the subdivision of units. It is the business of this officer to conduct the entire attack ; the most important part of his duty is to point out the proper direction for the main body to follow, as on this the success of his battalion will depend. If he undertakes in person the guidance of his advanced companies, those of his main body will be very likely to take a wrong direction, even to get quite out of hand (and this is no idle supposition, but an event of which there have been numerous examples in war). He must, therefore, confine himself to assigning a general direction to the advanced line, whilst he certainly will do well to leave the execution of details to one subordinate rather than to two. Then, again, the other available remedy, namely, that of giving the senior of the two captains in the front line the command of both companies seems insufficient, on account of the uncertain nature of such an ill-defined office—an office inconsistent with the custom of the service, which, indeed, admits of an officer taking over the command of those of like rank in rear, whilst the chief reconnoitres in front, but is very much opposed to the same being done under the actual pressure of danger and emergency.

Lastly, in order still further to strengthen our argument, we must allude to the possibility which always exists of the attack not encountering as stubborn a resistance as is expected, in which case the skirmishers do not require any strong support. In this case, also, it is doubtless more advantageous to have at first only broken up one company, instead of two side by side, into skirmishers.

There could be, neither in theory nor in practice, any fair argument to oppose to the formation of the skirmishing line under one sole leader; were it not for the second phase of the question, that of *reinforcements.*

Now, considering the line of supports merely as such, that is with reference to their special task, it appears to us just as important for them as for the skirmishers to be under one chief. If with regard to the latter, the thing has a more positive significancy ; with regard to the former, the same is more of a negative kind. In practice, we so constantly meet with two conditions easily arising, which both combine to produce the same undesirable consequence, that it would appear, to say the least, expedient to discover something to counteract them. We mean that the skirmishers in front always wish to have the supports as near as

possible, or even up with them, and are disposed to
assert that they might have done wonders " if only the
supports had been closer ;" on the other hand, the
supports in rear are always anxious to give up their
thankless post of "bullet-catchers," and of their own
accord to join the skirmishers, whilst the mutual tendency of the two lines to unite is, no doubt, the
stronger, the nearer the relation between them.

This tendency, which with a view to an attack
executed with *calculated energy*, and not with *mere
élan*, should be in every way opposed, because it will
all too readily lead either to, what we have already
alluded to, the overcrowding of the skirmishers, or to
an immoderate extent of front, this tendency will be at
least weakened if the connection between skirmishers
and supports is made less intimate. In other words,
if in place of the captain who has rushed away to his
front division into the thick of the battle, we have
another captain to influence the support which is independent, and to be used only when he is convinced of
the necessity, the evils which we have pointed out
will be more easily avoided than with the other
method. The independent leader of the supporting
line being of course kept informed of the progress
of the fight in his front, whilst, on the other hand,
from his position in rear, better able to overlook
the situation of the skirmishers than one who is in
the midst of them, can judge more calmly and justly
of the time and place at which he should give rein-

forcement, and of the number of men to be employed, and as they are his own people, he will take care that his subalterns do not expose them prematurely to loss.

The *one* leader of the skirmishers takes the initiative; the leader of the second line has only to follow in the same direction; far from him be the temptation to take a line of his own. He must consider himself *the second drop upon the same spot in the stone which the third drop will penetrate.*

Perhaps it may be said, "So far so good; but now comes the moment when this support must actually be given, when gaps have been torn in the skirmishing line either by the enemy's fire or by an undue extension involuntarily produced by accidents of ground. These gaps must be filled up. What, then, must infallibly happen? Why, that one company will be doubled up with the other. Then what a medley; what disorder! And this will upset all your theories."

Before replying to this new objection we must go back and cast a glance upon the influence which some of our later considerations have upon the subject of the maximum front of attack permissible to a body of troops—a subject to which, it will be remembered, we promised to return.

We shall once more take the case of a battalion without supposing it to be fighting by itself. When an attacking line is composed of several battalions, those on the flanks have from the first no neighbours to keep them within limits; but in the case of the centre battalions also it may happen that the restriction to their lateral extension may either not exist from the first, or may cease in the course of the action.

Up to what point may, ought, or must a battalion thus placed make use of its freedom to extend ?

We leave out, as not here to be discussed, all mention of the tendency to turning and surrounding movements ; as presupposed, we have only here to do with a force whose objective is *in front.*

With regard to this we have already above stated, perhaps thus forestalling subsequent speculations, that a force of this nature should at least devote half its strength to the main body. We have also admitted the justice of the principle that the advanced line should be as strong and dense as possible, at the same time laying great stress upon the importance of being able to concentrate its fire upon the point where the enemy's line is to be broken. Lastly, we have noticed how necessary it is for each commander to have sole direction of the attack which he has to make.

From these three factors we may deduce the maximum front which a leader may allow his attacking line to take up, consistently with vigorous action. He may at the outside extend half of his force as an advanced (preparatory) line. This half may, in order to render the *preparatory* fire effective, and supposing it to meet with only moderate losses, increase its original front by perhaps two-thirds the space it occupies when extended, *i.e.*, for a battalion, from 300 to 500 paces.

The indispensable condition remains that the line should be able to concentrate its fire, which will always be practicable, that the ground should permit the main body to approach so near to the skirmishers as to be able to reinforce them at once, which may be doubtful; and lastly, most important of all, that the commander should be able to make his influence felt unmistakably from one extremity of the line to the other, which will always be difficult, particularly as he must dismount.   But as soon as any one of the above conditions is not complied with, the operation ceases to be calculated and directed on a fixed object; it becomes a mere chance affair.   Thus we fix the limits for the extent of front.

Now let us return to the question of *mixing up one tactical unit with another* (Eindoublirung).

The expression is objectionable, and it stands for a practice which is still more so, yet a practice which is now-a-days unavoidable.

If you had said to a tactician of the time of Frederick the Great : " It must come to this; every single foot soldier will shoot whenever he chooses and has the chance ; and the battalion, company, or platoon volley will be a thing of the past "—he would only shrug his shoulders with contempt for such "an awful state of disorder."

Nevertheless, the time has come when the army,

without disowning its old traditions, has got on very well in this very state of disorder.

May not the same thing occur in the matter of mixing up tactical units ? It is an undoubted fact that the practice of doubling in files out of their proper order (a greater innovation when made than any we have now to attempt) has already been adopted as a matter of regulation in the army, has been employed by generals with war-experience, and carried out by our recruits twenty, thirty, forty years ago. Cannot our present recruits also do as much ? To this it will be answered that the practice was abolished because impracticable ; and no one will deny that this was at the time a wise measure, because in their then existing state of development elementary tactics did not require the formation.

But now the state of things is very different. The practice of mixing up men out of their proper order is no longer to be avoided.

It is no longer possible for skirmishers within effective range of the enemy, and in face of the breech-loader, to take ground to a flank, or to diminish their intervals, without suffering fearful loss, hence nothing is left for a reinforcement coming up from the rear but to double itself up with the skirmishers.

We shall return to this theme once more when we describe the actual execution of the attack in which the bodies referred to will attain greater dimensions than in the case with which we are now dealing. But if it be once established that we cannot avoid the practice either on a large or on a small scale it would appear well to accept it frankly.

As the proverb has it, a danger once recognised ceases to be a danger. Well, then, on the same principle, *regulated* disorder ceases to be *disorder*. In the question now before us we do not then escape this conclusion—we must break up tactical formations either by mixing up the divisions of the same company together or by mixing one company up with another. We maintain that the latter measure is only in appearance worse than the former. If once the original distribution of troops in line of battle is disturbed, it does not much matter, during the heat of action (and we are only treating of that period) by whom the disturbance is occasioned. When such mixing up of men occurs in action, in those moments of danger and of excitement strained to the highest pitch, personal influence on its own merits will affect the soldier more than the influence of his immediate superior merely as such. He will follow the lead of the brave man, the hero, whether belonging to his own company or not.

It is in such moments that a superior officer, often entirely unknown to the men about him, will carry them away with him, and that lieutenants have gained their spurs with the aid of men whom they never came across before or since. In such moments, we assert, it does not matter whether the original order is disturbed by men of the same or of another body. But when the fight is o'er, when it is advisable to restore the original order of things after the momen tary disorder, this will be more quickly accomplished if only two units are in question instead of the fractions of one unit, for every soldier knows his own company; thus officers and non-commissioned officers quickly find out the men of their company in the crowd. But many a man may forget to which division (zug) he happens to be attached on the particular day, and the officer who knows the whole company by sight cannot be expected to remember whether John Smith forms part of his division on this occasion.

We do not deny that many and weighty arguments may be brought against the aforesaid. Nevertheless, after weighing one argument against the other, we are still inclined to propose the following principles for the *preparation of the attack:*—

1. In order to prepare the way effectively it is necessary to bring up your skirmishing line to between 200 and 400 paces of the enemy's position, and to overwhelm with a concentrated and uninterrupted fire the particular part of it on which you intend to direct your assault.

2. In order to do this, the attacking force should be divided into an *advance* and a *main body.*

3. These two bodies should be in such proportion to one another that from one-fourth to one-half of the total strength should be allotted to the *advance.*

4. The *advance* is again divided into skirmishers and supports ; the former bringing as many rifles into play as the nature of the ground will allow, the latter being intended to make good the losses of the former, must, on open ground, be of equal strength to them, but under favourable circumstances need only be half as strong.

5. The better the cover afforded by the ground the greater may be the extension of the skirmishers during their advance. The limits to be assigned to this extension depend on the necessity which exists of ensuring unity of command throughout the attack, and of being able to concentrate the skirmishers' fire upon one point. The front for a battalion of 1000 men will range between 300 and 500 paces.

6. For the sake of unity of command it will be advisable for every battalion taking part in the attack to form its line of skirmishers with one company, and its supports with another.

7. The skirmishers should advance from the extreme range of the artillery fire bearing upon them as far as the extreme *effective* range of the enemy's infantry in one body. The company which furnishes them should always be extended in one line before it becomes a target for the enemy's fire, even if at first it had formed some supports. This advance from 1200 to 800, if possible, to 600 paces of the enemy, takes place as long as may be without opening fire, individual firing by word of command being only allowed when you can

no longer dispense with its animating effect, or when special reasons for it arise (such as the necessity of driving in advanced parties of the enemy, &c.).

As soon as the line of skirmishers reaches the zone of loss from *aimed infantry fire* it changes its mode of progression to that of the alternate *rushing forward* and *lying down* of separate fractions.

As far as it is possible (the nature of the ground and the advantage taken of particularly favourable moments forming exceptions), these rushes are made by whole divisions, and not over more than from fifty to eighty paces at a time; whether in succession from a flank or chequerwise is immaterial. Each time, the divisions which are halted and lying down cover by a steady, well-directed fire the advance of the others. Only when the skirmishers have advanced to within the most effective range of the enemy—say from 400 to 200 paces—will an unmistakable command or signal be given, upon which a *rapid independent fire*, as much concentrated as possible upon a point previously indicated, will be opened and will be maintained until the moment of the actual assault.

8. The distance of the supports from the skirmishers and their mode of advance, will be regulated as provided for the portion of the attacking force, which remains in close order (see, further on, the *execution of the attack*).

9. The skirmishers will be reinforced by the supports, as far as practicable, by doubling in separate sections (such as "divisions" or "groups") between

separate sections of the front line; but the details of execution will always be subordinate to producing the best possible effect upon the enemy.

II. THE STAGE OF EXECUTION.

Whilst it was the task of the *preparation* to pave the way for the attack, the work of breaking the enemy's power of resistance by employing the greatest possible amount of striking power, devolves upon the *execution*.

In spite of all the preliminary work the assailant cannot dispense with this extreme measure, because, as we shall see, the defenders have considerable means at their disposal to support their power of resistance, both directly and indirectly, to such an extent that the *preparatory* force will only succeed in exceptional cases in rendering them incapable of further efforts.

Although we must needs return to this question, and treat it more at length, when we deal with the *Defensive*, we still cannot avoid reference to the *indirect* means at the disposal of the defender.

These means are;—fire intended to shatter and break up the *striking power* of the assailant before he is able to come to close quarters.

In the effect of this fire, delivered as it is by the defender from the halt on the assailant who is on the move, lies the great risk for the latter of seeing his numerical and moral superiority (whether original or acquired) demolished and annihilated. We must

study the nature of this fire if we wish to discover an
antidote against it for the *attack*, and the inquiry will
lead us at first beyond the domain of infantry tactics
into that of artillery.

Without wishing here to enlarge upon the employment of the latter arm in attack and defence, we must,
however, go so far as to point out that the attacking
force is not seriously endangered by the artillery of the
defender at the extreme ranges of which the latter is
capable, but only when it gets so near that the gunner,
who ought not to waste his ammunition on chance
shots, can see the object he is aiming at clearly, and
can mark the effects of his fire. If the defender's
artillery act otherwise, all the better for the assailant.

We need, therefore, only trouble ourselves with the
defender's artillery from the point at which (taking
into consideration the power of its present matériel), it
is able to have a fair prospect of hitting a mark of such
size as an attacking force is likely to present in the
first moment of deployment, supposing it to be handled
according to our present ideas of war.

Not to waste our time in sophisms by taking into consideration conditions of ground and attacking masses,
such as would not actually be met with once in a hundred times, we may content ourselves with making the
following deductions from what has gone before : that
an attacking force composed of several battalions and
batteries (more than three or four), in line of columns
(Rendezvous Formation), will, without supposing con-

ditions of ground unusually favourable to the defender's
artillery, come within the zone of *aimed* fire at about
3000 paces from the enemy.

Conditions of ground favourable to the attack, and
other circumstances, such as dull weather, the smoke
occasioned by a fight which is already raging, &c., may
shorten this distance very much, just as, on the other
hand, circumstances may arise to lengthen it.   But as
we are here dealing with average chances for both
sides, we hold that, at a distance of 3000 paces from
the enemy an attacking force should form line of battle,
and should in most cases, reasoning from what has
already been adduced, go straight to the point.

The advanced troops begin the action supported to
the utmost by artillery, if possible superior to that of
the defenders.   Though we have here only to do with
infantry tactics, we must needs take notice of a moment
when support from the sister-arm is so necessary and
important—even, it may be said, decisive.

From this moment up to that of actual collision the
assailant is exposed to two kinds of fire-effect—that is
to say, to that of *aimed* and *chance* shots, a distinction
which has perhaps hitherto not been as much noticed
by enquirers theoretical and practical as is required for
the solution of the question of formation.   The artillery of the defence, and soon also its infantry, become
the objects of the assailant's fire.   Thus the chief attention and chief efforts of the defenders are in great
measure distracted from that portion of the assailant's

force upon which the actual execution of the attack will devolve. The more the advanced troops of the assailant succeed in doing this the better for his prospects; and, on the other hand, the defender will do well to resist the temptation. Nevertheless, his fire will be of some use, if directed, not on the front line of skirmishers, but on the supporting line and batteries. Its effect upon the main body will be at all events secondary and accidental. Thus we see that if the fire of the defenders does not prevent the strong advanced line of the assailants from approaching their position, it runs the risk of being silenced by the latter, and that if this fire is, on the other hand, concentrated on the advanced line, the progress of the main body will be thereby indirectly facilitated.

The possibility of success for the *Offensive* is founded upon these contradictions so difficult for the *Defensive* to reconcile, and in order to take full advantage thereof the advanced line of the assailant should be a strong one, for the main body will thus be exposed to smaller risks. In speaking of the *preparatory* stage, we have already given our reasons for requiring that the advanced line should represent from one-third to one-half the total force. It should have in addition the whole disposable artillery.

Thus we come to the following result: that the advanced troops of the assailant will, and can alone, taken as a whole, be the objects of the defender's fire;

and that, up to the moment when it dissolves itself
into one mass with the advanced line, a moment which
must come sooner or later, as we shall see further on,
the main body will only suffer loss more or less accidental from the enemy's fire ; a rule which will only be
altered either by unskilful massing of the main body,
or by want of energy on the part of the advanced
troops and of the accompanying artillery.   The nearer
a second line follows a first one on which the enemy's
fire is directed, the greater share of its losses must the
former suffer.   It is therefore advisable to keep as
much distance between the lines as may be possible
consistently with the time required to bring those in
rear into action at the right moment. Now, in treating
of the *preparatory* stage, we have already found that
from the moment when the advanced line begins its
rapid independent firing, the main body should not be
more than 500 paces in rear, if it wishes to arrive in
time.   And the distance between the lines cannot be
allowed to be much greater even during the period of
advance which precedes the *rapid independent firing*.
The arguments in favour of maintaining unity of command of troops making an attack on one object, in
respect of depth, that is of the advanced and main
body being under the same leader, have been partly
given already ; and as we have established that it is a
condition indispensable to this unity of command that
the front should not exceed 500 paces, we must now
likewise assign the same limits to the depth, limits to

be, as a general rule, not materially exceeded without exposing the commander to the risk of losing control over one or other half of his force.

It must therefore be a fixed rule that the main body of a battalion should in the first moments of the attack not keep more than 600 paces in rear of its first line of skirmishers.

As, on principle, there can be no check in the attack from the moment of its first commencement up to that of actual collision, without seriously compromising its chances of success; as however the advance in rushes and by fractions to which the front line is forced when under the enemy's effective musketry fire must needs delay its progress, whilst the main body, on the contrary, keeps moving steadily on, the latter will by the time the *rapid independent firing* begins have reduced its distance from the former to a maximum of from 400 to 300 paces.

If it now keeps moving on, as it must do, the time allowed for the *rapid independent firing* from the halt will not exceed from two to three minutes, but as there is still a space to traverse beyond the skirmishers of from 200 to 400 paces which cannot be crossed without the aid of the most intense fire, the *preparatory* force will have time enough for its task.

It remains to inquire, given the above-named distances between lines, how soon will the main body begin to suffer from the fire directed on the advanced troops?

The answer will be different according to the nature of the fire intended—that of infantry, or that of artillery. Whoever has taken part in an attack will testify that real danger for the second line begins with the rifle bullets, to which indeed mitrailleuse shot and an exceptional stray shrapnel may be added.

The modern infantry musket propels its bullets to the distance of from 1200 to 1800 paces. The individual infantry soldier on opening fire is not able to judge his distance accurately ; his misses are, and must therefore be, very numerous indeed ; and they will be all the more numerous the greater the distance at which he commences firing ; but all these ill-aimed shots render the ground lying behind the objects aimed at extremely dangerous to traverse, but dangerous to an extent utterly incalculable. Modern artillery, on the other hand, possesses much more effective means of controlling its aim, also of correcting it and of estimating the distance. But the peculiarity of its projectiles renders its misses only dangerous to the extent of the error in estimating distance, which experience shows us to be (and this is advantageous to the assailant) more often too low than too high.

That is to say, a body of troops following in second line will not suffer from artillery fire directed on the first line unless it come within about 300 paces of it ; but if the first line is the object of infantry fire, the second line will probably share its losses from the moment it gets within extreme rifle range.

It follows from these various considerations that in calculating how far the formation of an attacking force can contribute to guard its *striking power*, physical and moral, from being impaired, we have to divide the action of the main body into three stages: first, from the commencement of the movement to attack up to within from 1200 to 1800 paces of the enemy's position; secondly, from thence until close up to the advanced line, *i.e.*, to within 500 paces of the defenders; lastly, during the remainder of the distance. In the first stage we must aim at not affording so good a mark to the enemy's artillery as to give him a prospect of reaping great and undoubted advantage from aiming at it, thereby diverting his attention from our advanced troops, and especially from the artillery accompanying them. This same artillery, and the advanced troops moving on with its support, are at this moment much too threatening a danger to the *defence* for them to be ignored without very cogent reasons. If then the advanced line is strong enough, and if the main body follows it at not less than from 500 to 600 paces, it would appear certainly advisable to form the latter in columns of moderate size, with a front not exceeding from 50 to 80 paces, and a depth of from 25 to 30 paces (from 6 to 12 files), with intervals, if thought expedient, of about 100 paces. The marks thus afforded would hardly be attractive to the enemy's guns.

We come now to the second zone—that of *unaimed*

rifle fire. In attaining this the main body will pass
beyond its own guns, which have in all probability
advanced so far to prepare the way. To the chance
hits of the defender's infantry are now added those of
his artillery, whether the shots are aimed at the assailant's guns and fall short, or at his advanced line
with too much elevation. If their attention is not
fully occupied by the advanced line, the enemy's
gunners will from this moment onwards take as their
mark the main body which is gradually approaching.
At this period, the fire, both aimed and unaimed, will
be so intense upon the whole space, but at the same
time (unless led to concentrate itself by the assailant's
adoption of particularly unskilful formations in mass)
so equally spread and in a manner so impossible to
calculate, that in whatever formation the assailant
advances along the whole front, as long as he avoids
too dense bodies, his losses will remain much the
same.

We decidedly assert that it is neither necessary nor
will it be of any use to try and invent tactical formations calculated to diminish loss at this stage of the
proceedings; rather is it possible and expedient to
search for formations tending to weaken the moral
effect which the inevitable losses are sure to produce,
and thus *indirectly* to contribute to the *striking power*
of the attack that assistance which these formations
cannot give *directly*.

Great losses bring the attacking force to a standstill,

because even those who remain unwounded are dis-heartened by the sights which meet their eyes, and are likely to lose all hope of success.

When troops engaged in making an attack are brought to a standstill, in a very short time they begin to retire, that is to say, the attack fails.

But to overcome this fit of faint-heartedness is really the task which one formation more than another may favour.

Allowing that officers, non-commissioned officers, and individual soldiers, endowed with remarkable physical or moral courage, are those who will influence the masses and carry them away with them in such moments of weakness, one might be inclined to say that the more densely the mass is packed together, the more will the consciousness of strength be developed in it, the more plentiful will be those strong elements within it, and the more easily can the conduct of those setting a good example be witnessed by all, thus imparting the desired impulse to the mass.

One cannot deny that there is much truth in these arguments, and thus in other days the column forma-tion was adopted specifically as that of attack. On the other hand, however, it is objected that serious losses suffered at the same time and place have a more depressing effect upon the imagination than the same amount of loss would have if spread over more time and space ; so that it may be said that the less densely a given number of men are massed, the less will they

F

require the example to carry them on. Let us make a comparison. Take a column of 400 men—a front of twenty file, a depth of twenty ranks, with intervals of about a pace between them. A shell falls well into the mass, and knocks over perhaps eight or ten men. Well, the moral effect of this upon the whole body will be much more serious than if these same 400 men had been drawn up two deep, with intervals of two paces between the files. Three or four shells may fall amongst them at the same time, but in different places ; one man may be knocked over here, two there, three in another place : perhaps on the whole as many as in the column ; nay, even more. Still the effect upon the survivors will be much slighter.

The example will be all the more forcible in the case of shrapnel, on account of the small lateral dispersion of the bullets ; yet no one will deny that in both formations the losses will be, as above represented, about equal, however highly the practical result may be estimated.

So the question of formation reduces itself to this— where to draw the line between dense masses and open lines.

But, besides the actual and moral effect of the enemy's fire, we have to consider another agent having influence on the solution of the problem thus set before us. The desired formation will not be one suited to standing still, but to movement, and to the greatest possible development of fire at the end of that movement.

And there are other requirements to be satisfied besides the purely negative one of not interfering with the action of firearms. The formation should be as favourable as possible to forward movement, and it should not require to be changed when you come to close quarters.

The forward movement will be favoured both directly and indirectly by the *broader front and lesser depth*, as nothing is more fatiguing or trying to men than to march in a dense mass one behind the other; and nothing is more damaging to the moral influence of the leader, who must, as things go, be always at the head of his troops, than to have to diffuse it from front to rear instead of to the right and left. He has not the same power of superintendence, and his example has less effect.

In like manner a broad front and small depth are favourable to the use of firearms.

Thus both requirements act in the same direction as the tendency to the more extended order; and though this may perhaps be obtained just as well with a deep as with a broad formation, yet we must still remember that its most important quality—that of concealing the inevitable general loss as much as possible from the observation of the attacking troops—is only feasible with a broad front, in the case of troops who, as we are assuming, are constantly moving onward and leaving their dead and wounded behind.

The only things which tend to moderate this de-

cided tendency to spread out are the arguments already
adduced in favour of close order, and in addition the
general desire, natural to the party on the offensive,
to possess the numerical superiority—that is to say,
masses—at the decisive point; also the circumstance
that extension of front cannot be carried beyond
certain limits without dangerous results to the forward
movement; all which considerations are in favour of a
certain depth of formation.

Thus the question once more takes the following
turn: What extent of front should be allowed, and
what depth *can* be allowed to the main body at this
stage of the attack?

Our answer is: the extent of front should be such
as admits of the personal influence of the commander
being fully exerted (remember that he is now on foot);
the depth can be such as, without hindering movement, is yet sufficient to give the soldier the confidence
and solidity to be derived from the feeling of com-
panionship and from the idea of numbers—perhaps a
front of thirty or forty paces, with a depth of six or
eight files.   Between these little columns may be
intervals equal to or double the front of each.

We have thus brought the main body of the attacking force through the first zone in half-battalion columns,
through the second zone in company columns, and we
must suppose them close up to the advanced line.   It
remains now to revert to the supporting line of the
advanced troops (the company), and to study its opera-

tions during this period; for, when treating of the *preparatory* stage of the attack, we dealt with the general task which devolves upon it, not with the way in which that task is performed.

We have already mentioned that the advanced body of the attacking force will, and must be from the commencement, the object of the defender's fire, being at that time the greatest source of danger to the *defence.* As long, indeed, as the advanced line is unable to open fire, the enemy's artillery will prefer to play upon the main body, which offers a better mark, and which, at that period of the attack, is solely bent upon reducing the risk to itself by the covering fire of its own artillery, and by increasing its distance from the advanced line.

The latter, meanwhile, must, from the moment it comes within range, take care to adopt such a formation as will weaken the effect of the defender's fire, both actual and moral; for it cannot reckon upon any of the assistance which by its presence and action it, in this respect, is able to afford to the main body.

The considerations which, in consequence of this, weighed with the main body in its mode of traversing the second zone will have governed the advanced line already in its passage through the first zone.

These considerations, which were founded upon the feeling that it is desirable to advance in as broad and open a formation as possible, were all the more easily acted upon by the advanced body; because the objections to which in the case of the main body some force must be allowed, in consequence of the necessity of preserving the striking power, had not here the same weight.

The action demanded of the advanced line is simply that of its firearms, the effect of which can well be concentrated, even if the front is broad, whilst its composition, as above recommended, of independent parties placed behind one another, is more calculated to overcome the moral difficulties of the situation than is that of the main body.

The formation of the line of skirmishers is all that can be desired or expected; they have, besides, the advantage that their own busy action occupies their thoughts, and makes them treat difficulties more lightly (such is human nature).

But the supporting line requires more external aid, because it has not the benefit of the last-named indirect assistance.

Thus its formation must be such as not to offer a good mark for the enemy's artillery, which, we may assume, will at first have no better occupation than to fire upon it. It must, therefore, give up the column formation very early in the day.

Whether it will be best to deploy into line or to break into smaller columns, such as of divisions with a front of sections, may be left to each commander's discretion. Either formation will, with our present establishment, permit of unity of command as well as of free movement.

A second way of attaining the end is to regulate the distance of the supports from the skirmishers, which under artillery fire may no doubt be increased to 300 paces and even more.

In this manner the supports may traverse the first zone, and a good part of the second, without hesitation.

But the moment approaches when, the skirmishers having reached the most effective range of the enemy's musketry, the services of the supports will be in request.

The first condition for fulfilling their duties in this respect, namely, the nearer approach of the supports to the skirmishers, will be obtained of itself by the delay caused to the latter by their advance in successive rushes,—a course which, if possible, the supports must avoid. But in order to be in a position to give the assistance required immediately, and in the most direct manner, the supports must adopt the formation most suitable to a gradual but continuous advance.

The leader of the support should during this forward movement ascertain, as far as possible, where his assist-ance is most likely to be needed, and where it will be most effective, also the distribution of the enemy's bat-teries and other forces: the point chosen at which to force the position may be made out with some certainty at a distance of from 800 to 600 paces. The commander will then, as far as possible, assign to each of his parties such a task as he may consider the ascertained circum-stances to demand. As a general rule, to be modified

at need, these fractions of his command will be distri-
buted along the rear of the whole line of skirmishers ;
and whatever their formation may have been up to
this time, they will now assume that of an *open
line.*

We make use of this expression advisedly, to represent a formation which really is only that assumed at
the word of command to *skirmish.* But as the expressions " to skirmish," and a " line of skirmishers," are
very nearly allied with the idea of " fire-action " on
their part, and as such is by no means intended on the
part of our "open line," it would appear both expedient and necessary to make the distinction. We may
indicate the external difference between the two formations more precisely by pointing out that the files of an
open line do not "uncover," and that rifles are carried
at the slope.

The different fractions of the supporting line follow
the skirmishers in the formation indicated, from this
point, that is, on arriving within from 800 to 600 paces
of the enemy, and when the skirmishers begin the
decisive " rapid independent firing," establish themselves, as far as they have not already been obliged
to double up with them, as close behind them as
possible without intermixture. It follows as a matter
of course, that just as the commander of the supports has regulated their distribution along the front
at his own discretion, so he has also the power, and
must exercise it, to distribute them as to depth—for

instance, to keep back some of his parties so as to employ them at need in another direction. But in whatever manner the whole of this period of the attack may have been carried out, the rule holds good that when the main body approaches to within about 100 paces of what still remains of the line of supports, the latter throw themselves at once into the line of skirmishers, so as to give them the impulse necessary to carry them through the last and most dangerous stage, that of the *storm*.

We have already accompanied the main body close up to the advanced line. We have seen how the attacking force, starting from a compact mass, was at once forced to give way to a tendency to a more and more increasing extension and separation of fractions, and we have now reached the period when this tendency must again yield to that of concentration.

Before going further, however, we must most completely admit an *aim* which we have above purposely avoided acknowledging as a *principle*. We must do justice to the oft-repeated and defended demand that the main body also should move in *open line*.

It cannot, indeed, be denied that there are certain advantages in such a formation, which we also recognised in our examples of the dense and open order, but we cannot yet persuade ourselves that the great losses which we have all along declared to be as irre-

sistible as incalculable, are thereby to be really
prevented.

We do not, however, esteem the morally tranquillis-
ing effect of this formation so little as to wish to forbid
its being used *on the Commander's own responsibility*,
though we consider it specially applicable to the supports which are intended afterwards to skirmish, but
not suited to the main body, whose massive force alone
will tell.   In peace exercises, at least, we should not
willingly recommend it for use by the latter.

During the whole *preparatory* stage of the attack, of
which we have as yet been speaking, the companies of
the main body, whether ranged in column or in line,
having moved forward uninterruptedly, have arrived
close up to the first line of skirmishers.   The supports
which now, at the very latest, are joining the latter,
take part as well as they can in the *rapid independent
firing*, which has now reached its utmost intensity, perhaps pouring in their volleys over the heads of the
skirmishers who are lying down.   The commander
gives the signal for the attack, which is thenceforth
repeated and continued uninterruptedly along the line
by bugle call, and the whole line rushes forward as
rapidly as possible against the foe.   The little masses
of the main body follow, converging on any point
where the advanced troops have gained an advantage,
and have forced their way, pushing in like a wedge
twenty or thirty paces behind them.

There used to be a theory, not indeed yet quite exploded, according to which a storming party should attack *without firing a shot.*

We have accepted the distance of 400 paces as sufficiently close to the enemy for the advanced line of skirmishers to perform its task, considering the capabilities of the breech-loader of the present day; only under peculiarly favourable circumstances will it be feasible to reduce this distance to 200 paces. Taking then 300 paces as a mean between the two distances, we are to expect a mass, no matter how formed, to rush upon an enemy armed with the breech-loader for two minutes without firing a shot! But it will be objected, this is not intended; the skirmishers who remain lying down, and over whom the stormers pass without firing, have to keep up their fire with all their vigour, so as to support the column of attack. We reply, this is simply impossible unless quite exceptionally there chance to be flanking positions favourable to the attack, but which we must not here take into consideration in this study of a front assault.

Skirmishers who remain lying down, and who have to fire round the flanks and between the intervals of two or three little columns which are advancing beyond them, must cease firing when these columns have gone fifty paces to the front. The smoke will prevent their fire from being continued any longer without endangering the rear of the columns. Whoever has been in a position to hear bullets whistling past him from behind, even considerably on one side of him, though there could be no doubt of their being friendly bullets, will confess that such music is even less conducive to forward movement than is the rain of hostile shot coming from the front. But independently of these purely external reasons, which it must be confessed may not apply to some parts of a line of skirmishers when engaged in a front attack, the principle of leaving skirmishers behind you lying down is antagonistic to that main principle of the *Offensive*, that we should use all our available force in making an attack, and, moreover, it would do no good.

We have just established the fact that a line thus left behind can no longer use its fire with advantage, and the idea that it may perhaps serve to cover the shattered fragments of columns which have been crushed would be expecting too much after the previous exertions of the skirmishers. "*Forward*" is the word for them : to remain behind lying down is only a matter of theory; at the best it will be useless, generally even prejudicial.

All this, it may be said, never really happens; on the contrary, judging from war experience, we might maintain that the onslaught of the skirmishers would of itself suffice.

But here we are speaking of a seriously conducted and well-situated defence, so that, in theorising, we must keep in view all means which by any possibility may be useful, and in difficult moments must needs be and have been useful.

It is to be desired that the approach of the main body should impart a fresh impulse to the advanced line, tending to stimulate the forward movement which will culminate in the decisive assault. This last forward movement must be covered by as vigorous a fire as possible, which can, however, only proceed from the advancing troops themselves. Though it is doubtless true that this fire will not do much harm to the enemy, yet it must not cease.

The defenders, who are now threatened with the approaching assault, having been for some minutes the mark for the most intense fire, that which follows, accidental though its effect may be, as we readily admit, will not be without its influence on the morale of the defenders. (We have attributed a similar result from unaimed fire on the assailants.) At this moment, also, the artillery of the latter must be as active as possible to make up for the deficiency of infantry fire. What we have to do is to overwhelm the point of attack with as tremendous a fire as possible : we must not at this moment think of something to aim at ; on the contrary, the last stage of the *preparatory* fire will be most effective, if it prevents the defenders from daring to poke their noses out of cover.

The decisive assault having been thus prepared, executed, and supported up to the last moment, when we get to within twenty or thirty paces of the enemy.

we rush on with hurrahs and beat of drum, and may be pretty sure of the result.

You require uncommonly good troops (we shall have more to say about this in treating of the Defensive) to meet an attack in force, such as we have described, at this moment of its near approach, as it should be with the bayonet. We shall also see, that at this period of the engagement the success of the defenders will depend rather on efforts exterior to their own, that is to say, on counter-attacks made by other troops, than on their own stubbornness and tenacity—a circumstance of which we must say more when treating of the third stage of the attack. But having here only considered the attack of a given body of troops against purely defensive action, and having thought out the operation under those conditions, we have only to mention as a final requirement necessary to success, that the last decisive onslaught with shot and bayonet should be continued until the assailants actually reach the *further limit of the object of attack* (the further border of wood or village, the crest of a hill, &c.). On the other hand, they *must on no account go beyond those limits.*

The conditions, then, for successfully carrying out an attack, as far as they depend on the commander's dispositions, may be summed up as follows :—

1. Every independent body of troops intended to take part in an attack should have a distinct objective assigned to it by superior authority, and should direct

its efforts against this point, without cessation, with its whole strength and in the most direct way.

2. The troops must be deployed for the attack as soon as they come within reach of the enemy's artillery. They should be divided into a main and advanced body (compare chapter on the *preparatory* stage, page 53), the former keeping within 500 paces of the advanced skirmishers ; in open ground, and under favourable circumstances, nearer to them.

3. The support of the advanced skirmishers should, as soon as it becomes a mark for the enemy's guns, assume by degrees a more and more extended formation behind the skirmishers, first deploying from column into line, then spreading out so as to leave intervals between the divisions, and finally making each division expand into an *open line*.

The captain of the support will use his own discretion as to the reinforcement of the skirmishers, both with regard to time, place, and amount, establishing himself as close as possible behind them with whatever parts of his company remain in hand, and finally throwing himself with these remnants into the line of skirmishers to take part in the heavy firing, when the main body has approached within 80 or 100 paces.

4. The main body may get over the ground from first coming into action until reaching the zone of *unaimed* infantry fire, that is, until within 1500 or 1200 paces of the enemy, in little columns (either half-battalion or company), if the attention of the defender's

artillery is so much occupied by that of the assailant, or by his advanced skirmishers, that it cannot direct its fire on the main body.

5. From this point onwards, when either the mass attracts the fire of the enemy's guns or begins to catch his rifle-balls, it should resolve itself into company columns, with intervals of from 40 to 80 paces, in which formation as near an approach as possible should be made to the advanced skirmishers, say to within from 600 to 400 paces of them. During this advance each company may, at the discretion of its captain, either deploy or else form *open line* from division columns.

Other formations, such as, for instance, the deployment of whole or of half-battalions, the *open line* from a deployed company, the advance by sections or by files from a flank of divisions, do not seem advisable, because they all more or less hamper the forward movement, and interfere with the influence of the officers, without sensibly diminishing the losses.

6. As soon as the main body has arrived within about 50 paces of the line of skirmishers, now reinforced by the whole of the supports, the commanding officer gives the signal for the assault, which will be made by both advanced and main body together in double time (from 120 to 150 paces in the minute), whilst the drums beat the "*storm march*" and the bugles constantly repeat the call, as lively a fire as possible being at the same time kept up by the advanced troops during the movement, which continues thus to

within about 20 or 30 paces of the enemy, then termi-
nates in a rush at full speed with a cheer, and the position is carried. The advanced troops will generally
make it their business to envelop the point of entry
whilst the main body converges upon it and breaks in.

7. The troops which force the position must aim at
gaining the further border of it, so as to be able from
thence to pursue the retreating enemy with their fire,
and every portion of the attacking force will try to do
this without regard to their original subdivision into
advanced and main body. It will not signify if at this
stage portions of the main-body companies pass beyond
or mingle with fractions of the advanced companies,
which may yet be engaged with the enemy within the
limits of the post which has been forced.

An immediate rush forward beyond the border of
the position is altogether inadmissible. The assailant
will do much better if he at once prepares the point
which he has captured for defence.

However much every subordinate officer should endeavour to keep his people together, all should yet be
prepared, and the men should be ready and habituated
to perform any task which the necessities of the attack
may bring forth at a moment's notice, with whatever
force may be at hand.

8. As soon as the success of the attack may be considered complete, every officer must do his utmost to
restore order as quickly as possible in his immediate
neighbourhood, and by degrees throughout the whole

mass, in spite of the over excitement or reaction which will probably prevail.

III. THE THIRD STAGE OF THE ATTACK.

We hardly require theoretical argument or graphic description to prove that troops which have made an attack, as it necessarily must be made, in the manner above described, will have expended almost all their power for a certain time, and require a period of repose which should, at least, last until the disorder which, as we have already asserted and still confidently maintain, is inseparable from such operations has been to some extent remedied. This third stage has at all times been an extremely dangerous period for the assailant, a period in which the laurels which have just been won at the price of blood, have often been again torn from the victor by a counter attack of the enemy. Hence it has always been the aim and the task of the commander when making his general dispositions for the attack to provide for this moment of depression, and in examining this part of the question we come to this difficult point, the subdivision of the force into separate *lines of battle.**

From what we have already said the rule must be

---

* "*Treffen*," the original meaning of which is to "*strike*," applied here technically to the tool used to give the blow. It is difficult to render the term in English. "Line" does not express it, for a "Treffen" may be broken up into several lines. "Line of battle" does it better, and is perhaps sufficiently clear to render the meaning intelligible, but the expression is cumbrous.—(TR.)

accepted as permanent that the aforesaid subdivision should only be made with a view to that moment of weakness in the attacking force, and not with any idea of being able to renew an attack of the first line of battle made unsuccessfully, by that of a second line.

The first fundamental condition always holds good—that the attack should be conducted so as to be successful ; in consequence we are bound to bring up as great a force as we can to the assault, and to keep only as small a portion of it back as may appear necessary to overcome the temporary difficulties referred to. In order to take the measure of our need properly, we must first consider more closely the task which the force thus held in reserve will have to execute.

If the assailant only had to deal with the defender's mere power of resistance, there would be no exception to the rule of bringing as many troops into first line as the space would admit of being employed effectively. But the *Defence* will and must, at least unless ill-conducted, make use not only of its power of resistance, but likewise of that power of striking which is also inherent in it, and this action on its part will cause the greater danger to the *Attack*, the more nearly it coincides with the last extreme efforts of the assailant. In treating of the *Defensive*, we shall see that its counter-strokes will best be dealt at the actual moment of the assailant's last rush, or, at least, immediately after this, because the attacking force will then be in a condition most easily affected by the offensive return.

We have thus in this place to occupy ourselves with the means at the disposal of the assailants to meet this danger.   We have already pointed out that even beaten infantry is never entirely defenceless; it will therefore here be sufficient if we bring even a comparatively small force of fresh troops to the support of men who, although, as far as the outward circumstances of the moment go, not favourably situated for resistance, are yet under the stimulating effects which every attack, particularly one which has just succeeded, produces.

Unless we have to deal with a numerical inequality between the two parties which sets all theory at defiance, a reinforcement consisting of one-half or one-third of the forces engaged in first line may be considered sufficient at this moment; that is to say, the assailant need not keep more than from one-third to one-fourth of his total force in reserve for this third stage.

This conclusion certainly seems rather arbitrary, and examples may be produced from military history of cases in which forces even equal to those engaged in front did not suffice, and again of others where a very small fraction was enough.   But as we must fix upon some proportion as to numbers in determining a normal order of attack, we shall do well to abide by the rule above given, sanctioned as it is by our general experience.

Of course the commanding officer remains at liberty to alter details according to the actual circumstances of

the moment; only let this general principle be adopted
—always to put our *main* strength into the *first* line.
Moreover, the absolute strength of an attacking force
will, as well as its distribution, affect this question. A
single battalion which has to make a decisive attack
will hardly be able to keep anything back, whilst a
division composed of four regiments, each of three
battalions, can barely afford four battalions as reserve,
and, on the other hand, an army corps will often only
employ one of its divisions in first line, &c., &c.

We have hitherto spoken of the danger incurred by
the *Attack* in its last stage, and of the remedy, but we
must now look back to another danger which, under
certain circumstances, may be encountered even
earlier.

The more an attack is made up of independent portions side by side—in other words, the more extensive
its front, the more easy would it seem for the defender,
who is perhaps only making an appearance of maintaining the defensive, to concentrate his strength
against some point of the advancing line, to break
through it, and to put an end to the attack by this
very counter stroke. This danger naturally increases
as the line gets longer, because the difficulty of a
contemporaneous advance of all parts of it augments
in proportion to its length, and, at the same time,
the risk arises of involuntary gaps being caused,
which would tempt the enemy to make these offensive returns.

When circumstances appear to produce this danger, we must strive to provide against it by our order of attack, and we come thus to the result that a second and third *line of battle* must follow the first, the former being only *conditionally*, but the latter *always* necessary.

A second *line of battle* in this sense (taking for granted the existence of a third line) will only be necessary if the front of the attacking force is so extended that its fire will not range effectively from one flank to the other, and concentric action against the enemy's counter attacks from both flanks to centre, or from the whole line to either flank, is thus not feasible.

It is a strong point in the breechloader that troops armed with it can hardly be attacked successfully in front without proper preparation, and, as we saw just now how the *Defence* was aided by its inherent power of striking, so in this case we see the *Attack* assisted by its inherent power of resistance, in consequence of which the disadvantages arising from comparatively thin lines are more easily overcome than they could be in former days.

If, then, at this moment of danger to the attacking force (the risk of being broken through), there is a good prospect of support from a flank, assistance from the rear may all the more readily be dispensed with, as at the worst we assume the existence of a *third line of battle* prepared to throw its weight into the scales.

We may thus say that when the attack is made by

comparatively small bodies, whose front when deployed
does not exceed from 800 to 1200 paces, no *second* line
of battle (in the old sense) is required if a body of
troops follows in reserve to perform the part above
indicated as devolving upon a *third* line of battle. In
other words, an attacking force not exceeding the
strength of a brigade will be best formed in a first
line of battle, with a reserve following at a considerable distance, in the spirit of a third line of battle.
This will be preferable to forming two lines of equal
strength, with but a small distance between them.

But even where, in consequence of a greater front,
the support of a second line of battle cannot entirely
be dispensed with, a comparatively small body will
answer the purpose. It is merely a question of fill-
ing up accidental gaps by doubling in with the first
line, and thus taking part in the attack, or of opposing purely defensive action against the enemy's
counterstrokes (a course much favoured by the breech-
loader), until whatever reinforcements are needed come
into play from right, left, and rear.

It will therefore be sufficient in most instances, that
when a second line of battle is required, it should be
looked upon (unless circumstances, to be noticed
hereafter, should render this course unadvisable) as a
detachment pushed forward by the third line, which
should furnish it of a strength suited to circumstances :
better this than to weaken the first line by making a
detachment for the same purpose.

We will proceed to consider the specific task required of the body, which we call the *third line of battle,* so as to bring this question to issue.

Be it understood that we purposely chose the expression "third line of battle," in place of that which is, perhaps, more generally popular, namely, "reserve," because the latter term is easily convertible with the idea of *standing still,* a part which we do not in the least intend the body kept back as last line of the attacking force to act.

The most dangerous counter-attacks which the defender can make on the assailant are those attempted during the last stage of the attack, because the latter will be at that period most thoroughly exposed to the effects of the enemy's fire, hence making the nearest approach to that shaky state which his advanced troops have been trying to produce in the ranks of the defenders.

But these counter-attacks must necessarily be directed against the flanks of the attacking force, if the troops making them are still to derive any advantage from the fire of their comrades, which by making a front attack they would mask. Only when a flank attack is impossible will the defender deliver his counter-stroke straight to the front directly after the enemy has broken into the position.

In either instance, the assailant will depend upon his *third line of battle,* which must, in order to meet the first case, be strong enough and near enough to encounter the enemy's flank movements by a similar manœuvre ; whilst, in the second case, it will only act the part of an "outer"* reserve (a part which will be described more at length in our chapter on the *Defensive*) to the main body reduced for the time to a defensive attitude.

In both cases the *third line of battle* will find its best field of action on one or both flanks of the attack, and the same rule will hold good with regard to its third and most difficult task, that of renewing an attack which has failed. The theory of allowing the remnants of a beaten force to pass through your ranks, and of being afterwards able to oppose a successful resistance to the enemy, in other times led to the formation of two equally strong lines of battle, one in rear of the other, but it is certainly, now-a-days, a theory, and nothing more.

It is now only possible to cover the retreat of a beaten force from a position on its flank, a direction therefore which, as it has been shown, the main body of a third line of battle is bound to take whatever the nature of the demands upon it.

Another question still requires discussion. What should be the distance between the first, second, and third lines of battle ?

Our answer may well be founded upon what has

---

* By *outer* ("äussere") reserve the author means a body which keeps itself separate from that which it is required to assist, *i.e.*, does not intermingle with it, as do for instance the supports with the skirmishers whom they reinforce. —(Tr.)

been already said about this matter of distances : a second line should be kept so far in rear as not to come in for a share of the losses of the first line, *i.e.*, about 300 paces, and a third line should follow close enough to come into action at once when required, *i.e.*, about 500 paces in rear of the hindmost troops of the actual attack, that is to say, of the second line of battle, if there be one.

The *lines of battle*, as we have hitherto viewed them, may be looked upon as the *defensive* supplement to the *Attack*, an element which cannot altogether be dispensed with as long as the *Defence* contains within itself any *offensive* properties.

Although these lines may appear to be so far lost as regards the special task of an attacking force, there yet remains to them, under certain circumstances, a not unimportant place in purely offensive action, though certainly in a rather different form, and therefore in different proportions, to what was required of them in former days, when the second line was supposed to " pass through the first," or the latter was expected to "renew" the attack. After the first line of battle (the main force) has made a successful attack, it will be the duty of the second line to clear the interior of the captured post of the straggling remnants of the defending force, thereby allowing the first line to devote all its strength to gaining the further border of the position, a measure which on principle should be adopted. The duty of

pursuing the enemy will be assigned to the third
line of battle, the first line being, as we have already
said, not only dissuaded from doing so, but also
positively forbidden to join in pursuit, further than by
firing after the fugitives.

It appears, therefore, that depth rather than breadth
is required in an attacking force to enable it to perform the tasks demanded of it, and thus the question
arises of how the different fractions composing this
force are best kept under command.

Which is preferable, that there should be unity in
command in the lines of battle with regard to front or
to depth ?

We should say, taking into consideration the
different duties which we have shown above to devolve
upon the two lines, that as a general rule the second
line requires unity of command more in the direction of depth, and the third line more in that of
width.

This principle will not, however, be so invariably
applicable as to be considered an unalterable rule.
The tasks which the different lines have to execute
will differ so much according to the view taken each
time of the actual situation of the moment, that it
will be best to leave the commanding officer's hands
free

However much we may have dwelt in the introduction to this *study* upon the necessity and expediency of
establishing a more regular system of drill for the
operations thus treated of, we have now come to the

point where greater latitude should be allowed than has hitherto been done.

Let us have a fixed *system of drill* to suit the tactical unity of the battalion ; fixed *rules* to govern the united actions of several battalions ; fixed *principles* to guide the commanders of several independent bodies of troops taking part in one battle.

Thus we define the *limits* between drill and manœuvre : now when it comes to five, six or more battalions, these may be said to manœuvre, even if they are acting together in the most open plain with the most complete unity of purpose.

As soon as a body of troops on the offensive is large enough to be divided into separate lines of battle, it will be well not to bind it any longer by any fixed drill regulations.

These regulations include the question of command which requires to be left the more *open*, that is, to be decided more according to circumstances, the larger the forces with which we have to deal.   In the present state of tactics, drill regulations cannot be allowed to rule any larger body than a regiment.   Whether the brigade should be formed with its regiments side by side, or one behind the other, is the brigadier's business, whose decision is thus the first called for in a matter affecting the question of lines of battle, which we are now discussing.   In proportion as the body of troops increases in size, and as at the same time more regard has to be paid to the combined action of the other arms, the latitude allowed to the commander will also necessarily increase, which, however, does not do away with the need of fixed regulations respecting the original formation of these masses (" Rendez-vous formation ").

The following principles will be sufficient to regulate their general employment in the attack, with reference to its third stage now discussed.

1. An attacking force of more than two or three battalions must needs be formed in more than one line of battle, so as to be able to meet a counter attack of the enemy, the possibility of which must always be kept in view.

2. A second line of battle becomes necessary when the front of attack is so wide that a charge made against it cannot be met directly by the wings of the assailing force, namely, if the front exceeds the range of a rifle-ball, say from 800 to 1200 paces. A third line of battle is requisite to help the advanced troops to tide over the weak moment of reaction through which soldiers who have met with a stubborn resistance will naturally always pass, and of which the defender is likely to take advantage for making a counter attack either on the flank of the stormers as they advance, or on the position which they have just carried.

Therefore, whilst a second line of battle is only necessary under certain conditions, a third line can never well be dispensed with ; that is to say, we shall always find it advisable to keep back a certain portion of the first line to follow after the fashion of a third line.

3. From a quarter to one-third of the total force will usually be sufficient for a third line, and the second may be much weaker.   The former will meet the enemy's counter-strokes by acting on his flanks, and, according to circumstances, will serve as an " outer " reserve after the position has been carried, or will undertake the pursuit ; the latter will fill up accidental gaps in the front line, oppose a purely defensive action to the enemy's attempts to break through, or clear out his stragglers after the position is won.

4. The usual distance of the second line of battle from the main body of the first line will be 300 paces, so that it may not share the losses of the latter, whilst the third line will follow at the distance of from 800 to 500 paces, so regulated that it may be at hand when its support is required.

Whilst the corps composing the second line of battle will, in accordance with the duties required of them, be disposed so as to cover the intervals of the first line, those of the third line will be most advantageously posted on the flanks with a view to the part assigned to them, which, however, does not prevent them from being at first kept together in the centre so as to be available for use on either side.   But anyhow they must be drawn to a flank in the extreme case of having to cover the retreat of the first line after its repulse.

5. The combined action of the second and third lines of battle with the first will depend too much upon circumstances to become the subject of regulation.

It will generally be convenient to place the corps in second line, under the same command as those in front of them in first line, whilst the third line had better form an independent command ; but the commander of the whole force must have full discretion in the matter.

If this arrangement is made we cannot avoid, in a second line at least, breaking up the tactical unity of the battalion into two independent half battalions.

IV. SOME CONCLUDING REMARKS UPON DRILL.

It appears evident from all that has been said upon the attack, and the formations suitable to it, that the drill-book provides all that is required in this respect. We do not require to invent anything new in drill to suit our new tactics, only to apply existing forms somewhat differently.

If, however, as we stated in the introduction, we are to regulate our drill by the requirements of the battlefield, it is most important and necessary that certain of the formations already sanctioned by regulation which have hitherto been kept in the back-ground should be brought to the front, and *vice versâ.*

The decisive command has already gone forth from a decisive quarter ; for the new regulations say, " the normal battle formation of a battalion in the open is that of company columns ; the battalion column should be avoided; even second and third lines of battle

should adopt the former formation under certain circumstances."

The company column is recognised by the regulations
themselves as the basis of skirmishing, and experience
teaches us that we shall not be going too far if we add
to the above precept the following one : "Skirmishing
order is the normal fighting formation for infantry,"
whether in the plain or in broken ground.

*If these truths have become the foundation of our drill
practice, we may certainly be able to dispense with a
number of close-order formations which are still much
used, and which waste a great deal of time.*

Still, the all-important intention of our drill-practice
in what close-order movements we yet retain will gain
still greater force.

No one will deny that the more extended (individual)
order becomes our battle formation, the more important
will practice in close order movements become, as a
means of training, for the individual soldier.   Just
as the one order becomes more necessary to us, so
the other, at the same time, gains consequence.   The
value of the solidity of the battalion column, of
readiness in passing from one formation to another,
of individual dexterity increases in like proportion
to the necessity for change from the one to the
other form of battle under difficulties.   The so-called
" steady drill," that is to say, the habit of most complete order and subordination at any given moment,
will therefore gain importance from the new require-

ments of tactics, and whatever can contribute to this, by making our peace practice fit us for war, should not be thrown overboard—far from it.

Nevertheless it is quite true that *simplicity* is more than ever desirable in our formations. Their value as a means of disciplining and preparing the soldier for what is to follow does not arise from complication, but from sureness of execution. It would appear therefore desirable not to multiply formations, or to render those we have more difficult, but rather to strive after the greatest possible simplicity, which is sure to bear good fruit.

This brings us to the well-ventilated question of which is preferable, the two or three deep formation ? It would really be desirable that this question were settled once for all by regulation. We cannot undertake in these pages to give the *pros* and *cons* in this matter, but it appears to us certain that the arguments in favour of introducing the two-deep formation, which were of weight in their day (when volley firing was the regular mode of fighting of infantry), have now lost their value ; the line of skirmishers is just as quickly formed from three ranks as from two (for we need hardly quarrel about the five or ten extra paces which the men have to go over,* and the three-deep formation is just as serviceable as the two-deep in close order, if ever that should happen to be used in battle.

* In consequence of the greater depth of column ; the rear division being as usual sent out first to skirmish.—(Tr.)

On the other hand, whatever arguments have been in former days, and are yet brought forward in favour of the three-deep formation still retain their full force. If formation in three ranks were made the universal rule, the complicated formation of skirmishers would be simplified, and the perhaps preferable subdivision of the company into four parts instead of three (four half divisions) would ensue, and all this without making any innovation.

Having just supported our plea of simplicity by the foregoing proposal, it may seem inconsistent on our part to speak up for greater latitude being allowed by regulation in the instructions for brigade drills.

As we have already stated, nothing requires to be altered in respect of the *rendezvous formation*, nor of any movements beyond the range of fire; the prescribed formation, one regiment behind the other, suits best the probable order of the column of route and the question of space.

Only from the moment that the brigade comes into action, the commander should be no longer bound to adhere to the forms of the drill-book. After a brigade has taken its fighting formation it cannot be, now-a-days, when under fire, directed by words of command as per regulation; therefore it requires such forms no more.

It is in fact impossible, under existing circumstances, to fix upon a normal fighting formation for the brigade.

Every possible combination has been made use of

successfully in latter times, from that of both regiments side by side, with their battalions in three lines, to that of the deployment of all the battalions in one line. It would appear therefore judicious to allow the Brigadier even when at drill, to settle the *how?* we know how decisive are his *where* and *when*, and the *offensive* does not demand more in this respect than do the other phases of battle.

CHAPTER III.

ALL defensive action which aims at a decisive result is composed of two elements; resistance and counter-attack.

Where the latter element is wanting, the *Defensive* is, according to Clausewitz, the stronger form with only a *negative* object; here, however, we have to do simply with the *positive* object of victory.

The *Defensive-Offensive* aims at the same end as does the *Offensive*, but in a different manner.

Whilst the latter begins by shattering the enemy's powers of resistance so as next to destroy his capacity for fighting, the former attempts to obtain the same result by previously breaking the enemy's powers of attack.

The *Defensive* holds it to be easier to break the power of attack than that of resistance, and therefore begins by only warding off the enemy's blows; but if it desires to smash its adversary, it is obliged at length to make use of its own powers of offence, in place of those of defence which have hitherto been called into play.

The *Offensive* attempts to perform both tasks by means of the same form of action.

The main difficulty of the Defensive-Offensive lies in this change from one form of fighting to the other, and it was this very difficulty which caused us from the first to reject the general adoption of the principle of the *Defensive-Offensive* notwithstanding its advantages as they appear in theory.

This transposition is, with the result at which it aims, namely victory, dependent upon the fulfilment of two conditions ; first, that the assailant against whom the decisive counter-attack is to be directed must have previously been shaken both as to his power of attack and of resistance by the defence ; the latter result being by no means necessarily identical with the former. Even if the attacking powers of the assailant are so broken that he has to retire, it by no means follows that his powers of resistance are so much impaired as to make the success of a counter-attack certain ; for, as above remarked, a repulse does not necessarily put the attacking infantry "hors combat," and they will not always be reduced to the fragments of which we before spoke. On the other hand, if the powers of resistance of a body of troops are broken, their powers of attack are at the same time destroyed. The converse is not always applicable.

Should, however, the first condition be fulfilled, still the second remains equally indispensable : the counter-attack must catch the assailants *at the right moment,* that is, *just after* they have been thrown into disorder —a state to which, in any case, they must previously have been reduced.

We may safely assert that to do this *at the right moment* is one of the most difficult tasks which falls to the lot either of commander or of troops. We shall return to this subject later, when treating of the second stage of the *Defensive-Offensive.*

Let us first glance at the other condition, which is, according to theory, arrived at more easily by the first stage of the Defensive, namely, resistance, than by the attack. This condition is, your enemy's demoralisation.

Now, the arguments adduced in support of this theory are founded on two advantages which the *Defensive* is said to have over the Offensive with regard to the action of firearms (and this it is which can alone demoralise the enemy) : first, that the defender stands still to fire upon his opponent, who is in motion, and thus can make more of his arms, being able to choose his time, to fire more shots, and to take better aim ; secondly, that being halted, he can more easily take advantage of the ground which, now-a-days, is a matter of vast importance.

The above-named advantages next demand our attention.

It is not to be denied that the use of firearms in battle appears to require the combatant to stand still, because movement destroys all certainty of aim, and after all, the effect of fire consists only in the hits made by the shooter.

We have already pointed out in our first chapter what technical deductions have been drawn over and over again from this specialty of the Defensive.

This is our time to reply, that even with the best firearms, certainty of aim will only produce a sure and absolute result when both shooter and object aimed at are at rest, hence that, *cæteris paribus*, the attacking skirmisher gets the advantage of a standing mark to aim at, which, at least, in some degree, counterbalances the disadvantage of being himself on the move.

The superiority enjoyed by the Defensive in this respect is therefore founded less on the fact of being at rest taken by itself than on the favourable conditions under which fire can be brought to bear on the assailant.

Firearms only give the defender a decisive advantage when he can really make full use of them from beginning to end of the action, where peculiar circumstances, such as ranges previously marked out, ensure his aim, or where the favourable nature of the ground, such as being placed behind a defile, or being able to bring his firearms into play, tier above tier, enables him to take full advantage of his numerical superiority.

Wherever these conditions do not exist, the assailant's firearm, now-a-days, by reason of its great

mobility, quite equals that of the defender in efficiency.

All these conditions of fundamental importance
depend upon the *ground.*   We no longer now-a-days
reckon upon the arm of itself making up for any deficiency in this respect, as we might, for instance, if the
breech-loader were opposed to the crossbow.

The former, then, of the two above-named advantages of the Defence is simply supplemented by the
second ; the superiority of position over that of the
assailant assumed as at first existing, and which is, or
ought to be, doubled, in consequence of subsequent
measures.   In fact, it is the *position* which alone can
give to the *Defence* the superiority contended for, the
position so far as it favours fire-action *directly* and supports it *indirectly* by giving cover to the soldier.

The old teachers also recognised this truth, and the
right choice of a position was the chief subject of their
discourses on the *Defensive,* discourses which we need
only so far recapitulate as will be requisite for the purpose of inquiring whether any, and, if so, what modifications therein have been called forth by the new arms ?

A clear field for fire in front; good *appui* for the flanks,
strong defensive points within, space for free movement both in the interior and in rear, an obstacle in
front ; these are in general terms the qualities of a
good position insisted upon in all books of instruction
on Tactics.

It cannot be denied that as far as a passive resistance

is concerned, the conditions remain still the same, even with the best arms.

But we aim at something beyond this for the *Defensive-Offensive*, and then two elements of superiority are admitted by which the rapid, grazing and certain fire of the new arms combines with local advantages to favour the counter-attack which was indeed contemplated in the olden time, but was a work of greater difficulty.

The assailant must now, just as formerly, pass over a certain intervening space, and get up to the position if he means to carry it. Whilst doing so, he is now, on account of the greater range of firearms, much longer exposed to their effect than he was formerly, and at the same time the intensity of the fire is much augmented by its rapidity; if even his own improved armament to some extent counterbalances this drawback, there still remains a certain surplus of gain to the *Defence*, which has profited, if not to an overpowering extent as some would make us believe, at least considerably, by this addition to its strength. But this implies nothing more than that the *Defensive* can now arrive at the same result as that always aimed at with a smaller expenditure of force; it can in fact economise strength.

If in the present day a skirmisher can fire three times as far, as fast, and as correctly as he could formerly, it is clear that he can produce at least as much effect with his rifle as three men could formerly with their muskets; now, whatever number of men can in consequence be spared in occupying the position (of course not losing sight of the intention of retaining it if possible), is so much in favour of the defender's counter-stroke, and the latter, like an attack which it virtually becomes, never can be too strong.

To this direct advantage which, as we have shown in treating of the attack, is really not illusory, although it may not, as theorists maintain, increase in like proportion with the improvements in firearms, because these improvements also benefit in some measure the *Offensive*, an indirect, and perhaps, still more important, advantage is added.

We have already mentioned that according to our old theories, in the time of the old arm, the indirect aid of an obstacle in front of a position was indispensable. The delay thus caused to the assailant, and the power thus afforded of concentrating fire upon a few narrow passages, replaced to some extent those qualities of range, accuracy, and rapidity of fire which were wanting in the firearms of the past. But this very obstacle became a hindrance to the Defender himself when, in seeking a decisive result, he attempted a counter-attack; and this truth has been recognised by the old authorities.

The power of the modern breech-loader has freed the *Defensive-Offensive* from this incumbrance, and the theory of obstacles in front of a position may now be looked upon as exploded.

We arrive then at the following conclusion to this general inquiry ; the *Defensive-Offensive* is dependent on the nature of the ground.

The breech-loader has produced some favourable modifications in the conditions to be sought after in choosing a position, enabling, as it does, the defender both to occupy it with a smaller force, and to dispense with an obstacle in front, thus both directly and indirectly facilitating the necessary counter-attack.

But the necessity of really having such a position, an advantage not always to be gained, still remains the first and foremost condition for the employment of this form of action.

The *one* principle derivable from the foregoing, whereon to found instructions for battle, will only supplement those already given in the first chapter, and is as follows : the *Defensive-Offensive* is only justified when a commander finds a position so favourable to a passive defence that he may safely calculate upon shattering the enemy's power both of dealing blows and of withstanding them, although occupying the ground with a comparatively small force ; * and at the same time one which enables him to make his offensive

---

* We shall only speak throughout this chapter of the *relative proportions* of the troops destined for the passive defence, (as few as possible) and of those intended to make the counter-attack, (as many as possible). Definite numbers can only be given if we have particular ground in view. It is, however, as well here to remark that a position requiring more than at the outside the larger half of the disposable force for the passive defence is, in our opinion, a bad one, and that to be called advantageous it should be of such a nature that a commander occupying it with *Defensive-Offensive* views should be able to devote about one-third of his force to purposes of resistance, and about two-thirds to those of counter-attack.

returns at the right moment, to make full use of his forces for the purpose, and to have the power of pushing the movement beyond his own lines.

We will now proceed to examine more closely both stages of the *Defensive-Offensive.* As we assumed in treating of the *Offensive* that the decisive point of attack was rightly chosen, so we now shall take it for granted that a good position for defence has been selected ; we have only to do with the modern conditions upon which a successful result depends.

1. THE STAGE OF RESISTANCE.

The *stage of passive resistance* is, in the first place, to the *Defensive-Offensive,* what the *Preparatory stage* is to the *Offensive ;* it serves to shake the enemy's morale. But, in the next place, it must be continued for a certain time, long enough, indeed, to prepare the change from one form of action to another, *i.e.,* to make the counter-attack possible, so that meanwhile the defender must at least be able to hold in check the enemy's power of attack by his own power of resistance.

The task of *Defence* thus divides itself like that of attack, into a preparatory and a principal period of action.

If the defender has to perform this double task along the whole front of the position chosen, it is very evident that such a display of force would be required as to exceed what will be presumably available, all the more because that on principle a minimum only can be employed for defensive purposes without compromising the success of the offensive return. We are not called upon to consider here the case of a *Defensive*, persevered in in spite of the defenders being actually numerically superior to the assailants.

The stage of resistance would in this case be so short, uncertain, and purposely designed to deceive (unless all tactical principles were set at defiance), that we need here lay down no rules for such a course.

We have only to deal with cases in which numbers are about equally balanced, or where, if there is a difference, the scale is inclined to the disadvantage of the defender.

Under such conditions in respect of numbers, it is evident that the defender cannot think of distributing his forces which are presumed to be scanty equally along the whole front, so as to be prepared every where for any possible emergency. He must, therefore, seek out other means of gaining his object, which means will really only be afforded by the position, if wisely chosen as it must always be with due regard to the force, though the choice must, to a certain extent, be independent of this consideration. The mode of occupying the position, which it will be for the defender to settle, will always exert a certain influence upon the means referred to.

It is a well-known advantage of the *offensive* which indeed contributes to making it the stronger form of

action, that the *initiative* both of time and place falls to
its lot, giving it the power of surprising the enemy. To
compensate for this special advantage, the *Defender*
possessed, and still possesses a certain general initiative, by means of which (if only his position be strate-
gically good, of which we have nothing here to say), he
can, from the nature of the position taken up, attract
his opponent, and force him to advance in one or more
directions determined by and known to him beforehand.

Passive defence must then be restricted to these
principal lines of attack, which are entirely dependent
on the more or less fortunate choice of position, and the
defender must, at those points, endeavour to perform
his double task thoroughly, whilst at other parts of the
position he only maintains an attitude of observation.

Wherever these main lines of attack may be, the
strong points of the defence, *i.e.,* of the position, must
be, and being strongly occupied, they must and will infallibly attract the assailant to them.

If even there should be neither local circumstances
nor troops arrayed for defence to prevent the enemy
from penetrating between the separate strong points of
a position, these, if well chosen, will exercise an irre-
sistible power of attraction upon him, both because they
threaten him *directly* by their fire, and also *indirectly* by
the attacks aimed from them at his flank and rear, from
which he is not safe till he has mastered them.

The first necessity of the *Defence* then, if it means to

perform its task with its relatively weak forces, is *concentration on decisive points.*

To put the matter in a negative form, we may say that the *Defence* should never accumulate forces where it will not presumably be exposed to decisive or would-be decisive attack, where in fact the assailant will probably only make demonstrations.

It being now established that the general principle of occupation of ground for passive defence is to concentrate on decisive points, and only to remain in observation elsewhere, we now come to the arrangement of details at these centres of concentration.

The nature of the case demands that every such centre should form an independent whole under one command, whose entire task amounts to this : to maintain himself with the force under his orders at the point assigned to him. Just as we said before, an attack to be successful and decisive should be conducted under the persuasion that "the sword severs or snaps asunder," so we may here require the defence to be maintained with the conviction that the "shield wards off the blow or splits." It has been remarked of the assailant that he never can tell what force he may chance upon, so now we may assert of the defender that he never knows but what he may yet be relieved.

The most determined and stubborn tenacity is alone capable of enabling the Defence to encounter the resolute energy of an attack, pushed to the utmost. The possibility of evacuating the post confided to him must be as far from the defender's mind as the idea of retreat from that of the assailant.

This appears to be a fit place to warn the student against conduct on the part of the defender corresponding to those premature and useless engagements which we denounced in treating of the attack: we mean the practice, for which the higher authorities are sometimes accountable, of maintaining and battling for points in advance of the actual position, which practice leads to repeated and long-protracted affairs of outposts (advanced and rear guard skirmishes, and such like). Here, as with the attack, we must insist upon complete clearness of judgment and will; the commander who wishes to fight a defensive battle, and has the opportunity of doing so in an advantageous position, must not, under any pretence whatsoever, expose a weak detachment in front of his position to the risk of being overpowered separately by a superior enemy, by this means lowering the morale of his army.

In the chapter on the "Temporising Combat," we shall speak of what must be done in this way as an introduction to the reconnaissance.

All this is a digression. Let us return to the one leader who has to hold one of the keys of the position.

The theory of our forefathers, which is after all the parent of our present wisdom, was in favour of the line formation for defensive purposes, just as it favoured columns for the attacking force. Modern views confirm these impressions. The whole power of resistance lies

in the complete development of the effect of firearms,
and substantially in this alone. But this maxim implies
the necessity of bringing as many rifles as possible into
front line, *i.e.*, the principle of the line formation. The
defender must strive to ensure to his firearms by all
possible means the superiority over any fire which the
enemy may be able to bring against him.

We have already touched upon the manner in which
a numerical superiority can be ensured in a confined
position (such as by concentration behind defiles, by
several tiers of fire, &c.), and it may be dismissed for
the present as belonging to the general question of the
choice of a position.

The other measure, that of ensuring superior accuracy of fire by marking the ranges beforehand, is mentioned here to be strongly recommended, although it
can only be carried out if there is plenty of time.

The third means at the disposal of the defender for
preserving his advantage, depends on time and place ;
we speak of cover, that is to say, reduction of loss to
the utmost, by taking advantage of the ground. Up
to a certain point, however, this advantage will always
be on the side of the Defence, because all ground
affords more or less cover to a man standing still or
lying down. The defender should never neglect to
add to this cover as much as he can by artificial means,
and with this view the rifle-pit is to him almost a *necessary of life.*

All these things, however, though of the greatest

1

importance, depend upon the conditions of the moment, as they may chance to be, upon the locality, the time and means available.   We have here more to do with the general principles which govern the employment of troops under all conditions.

In the defence of an assigned position, as in attack, this task divides itself into two branches, that of preparation, and that of execution.   Hence, the same as with the attack, as strong a force as the ground will allow must be devoted to the first task (being concentrated at the different strong points), at the same time, no larger force than can be employed with advantage ; that is to say, at a given part of the position, the first line should be from the very commencement as thickly occupied with skirmishers as there is room for, and, above all, as there is the power of bringing into effective action.   As these skirmishers are not required to move about, and as, further, they will as usual be posted under cover, they may be more closely packed than in the attack, without taking off from their efficiency, or exposing them to extraordinary loss ; and the following principle may be accepted, that troops employed in a passive defence will do well, whenever it can be done, to assign one skirmisher in first line to every pace of front.   The fire of this line should, as with the attack, be as much as possible uninterrupted, and here also we require a supporting line to make good losses.

Taking into consideration the more favourable

conditions with regard to cover, it will be sufficient if the supports be equal to half the strength of the skirmishers (first line). It is hardly necessary to remark that they should not actually join it till the attack has been clearly developed. The third part of the task committed to the passive Defence remains to be mentioned, and that is, to oppose its own powers of resistance to the whole striking power of the attack, at least until its own counter-stroke can be made effectually. We must describe the moment when this action will be required from the course pursued by the assailant as we have traced it.

The advanced troops of the attack have, thanks to superior numbers and greater extent of front, spread round the flanks and brought a concentric fire to bear upon this first line of the Defence, reducing it to silence; they then break in with their masses in one place or other, all their rearward troops being directed to converge upon it.

With comparatively narrow front, but hence more considerable depth, the stream of warriors pours into the breach.

To stem this torrent, the *passive Defence* requires a *reserve* or *main body*. We use the expression as we used it for the attack, but without reference to numerical strength.

Wherever it can be done, the reserve will use for its purpose independent *reduits* in this position, *i.e.*, strong points not yet affected by the preparatory operations of

I 2

the attacking force, and to carry which further *preparation* and another assault will be required. The possibility of doing this will, however, be reduced to a minimum by the range, precision, and destructiveness of modern artillery. Even in village-fights the inner *reduit*, unless exceptionally sheltered, will not be less cannonaded than the border, even before the actual assault.

Much less often than formerly will it now be possible to follow up the first period of passive defence by a second "interior" period. The fate of *inner* reserves will more than ever be bound up with that of the foremost line.

Much more frequently, therefore, than heretofore, will the *reserve of the passive defence* be forced to exchange its passive part of resistance for the active part of making partial use of its power of attack; that is to say, far more than in former days will even the passive Defence depend for success on assistance from the offensive element, which, in truth, was never strange to it.

·   We have already seen that an *Attack* well met by a *passive Defence* is not in the best condition to make its own power of resistance operative, and that even slight counter-attacks made at this moment, particularly if directed on a flank, will check the assailant, and will in any case prevent him from attaining his decisive objective, the "further border" of the position.

The passive Defence does not require an absolute preponderance of force to gain this end, because the assailant cannot at once develop his numerical superiority, nor immediately bring it into play.

The defender's best chances lie in surprising the enemy, in acting on the flanks, in displaying all his energy.

Be it as it will, however, whether the Defence remain entirely passive or whether it pass into the active stage, the struggle for localities, that real prototype of the *defensive* battle, will be decided in these days much more quickly than heretofore; the obstinate stubbornness of former conflicts of this kind will, with few exceptions, hardly be repeated in the same degree in face of the all-devouring breech-loader.

Hence it follows, that the *passive Defence* also depends less for the performance of the second part of its allotted task upon the numerical strength of its forces than upon their sudden action calculated to take the enemy by surprise, and therefore, in spite of the expression, "*main body*," being applied to the troops in second line the defender must always put his *main numerical strength*, as far as practicable, into the first line for holding the border of the position.

The relative strength of the advanced troops (skirmishers and supports), and of the main body (reserve), of the Defence will vary materially according to the position occupied.

In any case, however, the strength of the reserve during the stage of *passive Defence* should never more than equal that of the advanced body.

If, then, the defence be concentrated, as it should be, on decisive points, according to our reckoning three men per pace of the given front will be sufficient. This total again will be divided, according to circumstances, between first line and reserve, up to the extreme limit of 3 : 1.

We must further inquire what distance should be kept between the different subdivisions of the force which we have up to this time recognised as necessary.

As all movement under effective fire is undesirable, and as the moment when the defensive line of skirmishers will in all probability most need the aid of its supports, coincides with the period of most intense fire from the enemy (that of the rapid independent fire of his advanced troops), the general rule will hold good, that the support should be placed as near the skirmishers as possible, so as to be at hand when required. The disadvantage of such an arrangement is that it is apt to expose the supports to the same fire from which the skirmishers are suffering, particularly if opposed to the enemy's artillery (a disadvantage not always to be remedied by natural cover). The best way of meeting this difficulty will be, perhaps, by dividing the supports from the very first into small parties. The objection to this course, which was necessarily entertained when it was proposed for the *offensive*, that it leads to a too early intermixture of the lines, does not here apply, in consequence of the fact that both skirmishers and supports are lying still.

On the other hand, the first consideration for the Reserve is to keep as much as possible sheltered from the enemy's fire during the preparatory stage. A distance of from 300 to 400 paces from the skirmishers, varying, indeed, according to the nature of the ground, will generally suffice to save the reserve from being exposed to the risk of sharing the effects of the artillery fire directed on the first line. Again, as this body, even if acting straight to its front, should only come into play shortly before or contemporaneously with the enemy's assault, so that it may take the assailant all the more by surprise, the distance named does not appear too great; as an extreme limit the rule may be that the reserve should stand a little nearer to its skirmishers than they are to those of the enemy.

Naturally, however, these conditions depend entirely on the locality, and must needs be often considerably modified; for instance, in the defence of villages. The general principles which govern the distribution, strength, and distances between the several parts of a defensive force being fixed, we come now to the question of command.

It has already been established as a principle in our chapter on the *Offensive*, that unity of command is in direct proportion to the unity of the end to be attained, and to the possibility of the leader exercising personal influence over his troops.

Looking at the matter from this point of view, it would appear necessary that in a defensive force unity of command should reign in the direction of depth, as the arrangement most completely answering the require-ments of a stubborn resistance ; and we shall, therefore, here bespeak this unity of command unconditionally for skirmishers and supports, and for the main force in rear (reserve) also, if it can be posted within such a distance of the first line as to be visible to the com-mander of the latter (which, indeed, will not always depend entirely on the distance).

As, further, it is in the nature of the *Defence,* which cannot take the initiative at any special point, that it may become the object of the enemy's attack at any part of the position which he may choose to select, we should recommend dividing the reserve laterally into detachments independent of one another, and distri-buted in our general line at no great intervals.   The company column would appear to be a peculiarly suit-able formation for this purpose, and should, therefore, be the tactical unit of the *Defence.*

All this depends, as with everything connected with the *Defence,* very much on local conditions, which in the direction of width may easily be so similar throughout, that unity of command may be desirable, and, at least in the case of a battalion, may exist.

Without any intention of fixing upon a normal fighting formation for a battalion on the defensive, which would be unpractical, in consequence of the

great variety of possible situations, but rather to
illustrate the ideas which we have just expressed, we
shall, therefore, say, that a battalion, of course supposed to be in connection with others, and intended
to fight defensively in open ground, occupying, let
us suppose, the ridge of a hill, should spread out
its four companies with intervals of from 80 to 100
paces; each company (200 rifles) will extend one
division as skirmishers with a front of 80 paces,
posting about 50 or 100 paces behind these a half-
division (eventually broken up into sections) as supports, and establishing the remaining one-and-a-half
divisions, either deployed or in half-division column,
in *open line* from 300 to 400 paces in rear of the skirmishers : or else, a battalion to which the defence of
the border of a wood, village, or such like is entrusted,
and which need only provide for the enemy's reception
at certain fixed points of entry, will, according to the
estimated number of such points, place its companies
across them (an arrangement always far preferable for
the defence of a barricade to that of occupying sections
of the front from street to street), and will keep back
one or two of them (according to circumstances) as
reserve in close order, whilst the two or three companies fighting in first line are extended as skirmishers
and supports.

The circumstance that the force of resistance, for
entirely mechanical reasons, increases in the ratio of
the depth of formation opposed by the defender to the

attack directed against him (a circumstance which influenced us when we advocated unity of command in the direction of depth), brings us by an entirely different route from that pursued when discussing the attack to the question of *lines of battle;* and notwithstanding this difference, the ruling idea remains the same here as there, that of the lines of battle assisting the combatant to tide over the moment when we may presume that his powers of resistance will be put to the test.

In our foregoing treatise on *passive Defence* we have designedly, and on principle, made use of the expressions "first line" and "reserve," instead of "advanced" and "main" "body," which we employed in treating of the attack, in spite of the many points of resemblance indicated. In fact, when the *passive Defence* has reached the point of bringing into action that part of its force designated the "reserve," it has done its utmost, it has acted its part, that of holding its ground with all its might to the end. This element of endurance appeared to us to be best rendered by the expression "reserve," and just because this term implies an extreme degree of passive tenacity, we avoided it when dealing with the *Attack*. The well-known phraseology of all our text-books agrees with this our method, as they all have long ago applied the term "inner reserve" to the portion of the defending force of which we are speaking, at any rate, when they treat of local defence.

Inversely, we shall again, for the same reason, when speaking of the body of troops which delivers the counter-stroke of the *Defensive-Offensive*, not call it a " reserve."*

But now it is evident that if, as may happen in spite of original economy of strength, the numerical proportions of the troops employed in this *passive Defence* have assumed greater dimensions at the different points of concentration than we have presupposed in our general remarks, the subdivision hitherto imagined into skirmishers, supports, and reserves will be insufficient.

When, as has frequently happened, and as will often happen, in decisive battles between the great masses of the present day, the part of *passive Defence* devolves upon whole brigades, divisions, even corps, until other forces undertake the counter-attack, the question of distribution into *lines of battle* must needs crop up even from the point of view of space, when dealing with such large bodies.

In contrast to what was said in the chapter on the *Offensive*, the expediency and necessity of forming a second *line of battle* will have much greater weight in the case of the *Defence.* In the former case we saw it intended only as a stop-gap to be used in the impro-

---

* It may, perhaps, strike the reader that too much importance has often been assigned in this study to particular forms of expression which may be in fact synonymous. We are not of this opinion, as we have before mentioned, but think that the want of clearness in forms very frequently engenders a vagueness of ideas.

bable event of the first line being broken through by the enemy, or in the accidental event of a gap otherwise arising. But with troops engaged in a *passive Defence* this condition presents itself differently to the view.

Accidental gaps will certainly rarely arise, as every one is standing fast; but, on the other hand, the enemy right earnestly intends, and strives with all his might, to make breaches in the line, bringing all the weight of his powers of offence to bear upon the points assailed. The event which on the side of the *Attack* we have seen was an improbable *exception*, only to be provoked by the assailant's own faults, will, on the side of the *Defence* be the *rule*, and the object contended for by the enemy with all his means.

This circumstance at once renders a second line of battle uncommonly important to the *Defence*, even when the front is comparatively short, and in proportion as the line becomes longer, and, as thanks to the enemy having the initiative, the uncertainty as to his intended point of assault increases in like measure, so the value of a second line of battle is largely augmented.

The more total the defeat which would be entailed upon the defender by the loss of his position, the more speedily must reinforcements be brought up at need. It does not much matter to the assailant when met by a counter-attack of the enemy, at what particular point the same is made, as his resistance does not depend on the position in which he happens to be at the moment. Very different is the case of the *Defence*, whose position is the base of its strength.

If the *second line of battle* on the Defensive-Offensive side is called upon to cover the retreat of the first, we may look upon the game, taken as a whole, as lost, and probably definitively so.

Such are the principal reasons for the necessity of a second *line of battle* in a defensive position of some extent.

Like everything else on the side of the defender, the questions of strength, distance, and command of such a second line, depend entirely on the nature of the ground. The more this is favourable to the first line of battle, the weaker naturally may the second be ; we may, however, assume, that even in a position occupied by only one regiment, a second *line of battle* will be requisite, whether fighting on open ground or in woods or villages.

This second *line of battle* may, according to circumstances, be fused with the main body of the first line into one "inner reserve," or by relieving it make it free to act in front, or else itself operate independently as an " outer reserve."

It will not be necessary, after what we have already said in our chapter on the *Attack*, about *lines of battle*, and after what has elsewhere been remarked about the employment of reserves, to enter specially into the mode of action of the second *line of battle*, or to describe its conduct, according to circumstances, offensive or defensive.

What more remains to be noted under this head will be referred to when we come to the second stage of the *Defensive-Offensive.*

True to the principle, that even the most passive resistance must not remain without some infusion of the offensive element, the greater the force employed in the *passive Defence,* the more must the action of its second, eventually of its third *line of battle* (even if merely local, and therefore indecisive) be that of a force executing a decisive counter-attack; in fact, to do this should be its aim.

Having thus thrown some light on the question of the distribution of strength during the stage of *passive Defence,* it only remains to notice briefly the course which the struggle of the contending forces must take with the formations adopted by *Attack* and *Defence.*

We must at this stage of our inquiry first of all speak of the defensive artillery, which has not been hitherto mentioned, for without its assistance we cannot hope now-a-days to maintain a defensive fight on a large scale.

We shall start by assuming that the defensive batteries are placed in the most favourable positions possible, that they are, as far as can be, behind natural cover, and so forth; and that they are in the general line of the reserve, *i.e.*, about 400 paces in rear of the foremost line of skirmishers.

As certainly as it is inconvenient for the attacking force to be compelled to deploy at a long distance from the enemy, so it is clearly incumbent on the defender to force the assailant to this deployment, but it remains a question whether this task should, as a rule, be allotted to the defensive batteries. It is, after all, more important that they should catch the assailant at a really effective range, to ensure which they should not unmask themselves too soon. It would appear preferable to hand over this duty to an advanced party * of the *Defensive-Offensive* force supported by cavalry and some light batteries; in like manner, on the other side, the advanced guard of the assailant will endeavour to save the troops coming up from the rear from being forced into an unnecessarily early or inconvenient deployment.

The batteries in position should only open fire when the enemy is within easy range and there is promise of good effect (the assailant's want of skill may, of course, expose him to serious loss at an unusual distance), and should aim, as a general rule, at the attacking infantry, although they cannot be expected to resist taking advantage of the favourable moment for firing at the enemy's guns as they come into action.

But from the instant when the attacking infantry itself opens fire up to the very last moment, the defender's guns should never leave it alone.

The assailant's artillery will, in consequence of this

* " Einleitungstruppe," literally *introductory* force.

proceeding, be obliged to come nearer, and the defender's infantry must be left to encounter it, and to keep it at as great a distance as possible.

We have already mentioned as one of the qualities of a good position, that it should offer a clear field for fire up to the furthest effective range. We do not mean, however, that this should be taken advantage of from the first by the mass of the defender's forces.

Nevertheless, just as in speaking of the attack we dwelt upon the expediency and utility of even unaimed fire at the last moment, we feel ourselves obliged here to advocate *chance* shots on the part of the defence. The advantage of a range exceeding the length of vision of most skirmishers which the new arms possess ought no longer to be neglected for the purposes of *passive Defence*, in spite of all the value which we most decidedly attach to the fire of the masses at the most effective ranges, and only at such.

The moral effect produced upon the assailant by the whistling of hostile bullets, coming from positions of which he can as yet see nothing, is not to be undervalued (we have already referred to it when speaking of the attack), and every, even the smallest deduction from the moral force of the assailant contributed to by the defender, is of great value to the latter.

But certainly the remedy would become dangerous, and would produce the reverse of what is intended if administered in too large doses. Such unaimed fire can only, of course, produce mere chance hits, which

must be out of all proportion to the number of cart-
ridges expended. Now if the men of the attacking
force remark that out of the crowd of whistling bullets
not only some, but by far the greater number hit no
one, this sort of fire will encourage more than it will
depress. All the same, experience has led us to take
count of these chance shots in considering the formations for attack, hence we shall do well not to neglect
this means of annoyance. If some quite small detachments are pushed forward from the flanks of a position
or in front of it, and keep up a steady continuous fire,
well-regulated by the officers at ranges of from 1800 to
to 1500 paces, for instance, in the ascertained direction
of the enemy's general advance, it must at least somewhat influence the formations of the attacking force.
And as we have before remarked, the *passive Defence*
cannot afford to neglect even the smallest means of
offence. The way in which afterwards the real fire of
the masses, and lastly their rapid independent fire is
regulated, stands out in sharp contrast to the foregoing
proceedings. Fire should only be opened by the
defender's actual line of skirmishers at the range most
effective according to the mark aimed at, and should be
maintained with a certain degree of spirit without at
first taking the form of *rapid independent firing,* which
should, however, be practised when the object is to
keep the enemy's advanced line as far as possible from
the position, when preparing to open its own *rapid independent fire.* Success on the part of the *Defence* at

K

this moment causes most frequently the failure of the attack, as is well known.

But the defender develops the full force of his fire, bringing it to its highest pitch by employing supports, often also reserves, even his second line of battle at the moment when, as above described, the enemy advances to storm the position ; for the *Defence* truly the most trying time, but also the moment when all the commander's resources (arising both from previous training and momentary impulse) must be called into play, to awaken the firm conviction in his troops that to retreat *now* would be certain *ruin*, and that, as a last resource, they must take to the bayonet.

We may then resume what we said upon *passive Defence* as follows :—

1. The *passive Defence* must, in order to reserve as much force as possible for the decisive offensive return, endeavour to perform with a minimum of strength the double task of shattering the enemy and of holding the position.

2. Whilst the choice of position has much to do with the successful performance of this task, the mode of occupying it will also materially affect the result.

The troops employed in the *passive Defence* should be concentrated at points previously recognised and indicated as keys of the position, unity of command being preserved at each of these points, whilst the intervening space should only be observed.

3. The principle of the line-formation will govern the

disposition of the troops at each point occupied, *i.e.*, as many rifles as possible will be brought into action in first line.

One man to a pace in this line of skirmishers will best meet this demand, and a line of supports half as strong as the first line, and approaching as close as practicable to it will be sufficient, as it is assumed that both lines are well under cover.

Upon these two bodies, forming together the first line of the Defence, and which should also invariably be under one commander, devolves the task of shattering the assailants' power of attack.

4. So as under all circumstances to be able to hold a position once occupied, this first line needs a reserve (main-body), varying in strength according to circumstances, from equal to down to one-third or one-fourth of its own·numbers; this reserve serving *passively* to garrison a *reduit* or to furnish active support, under one and the same, or under separate command, according to which part it plays, but never more than from 300 to 400 paces in rear.

5. Unity of command in the direction of depth is desirable as long as the reserve is visible from the position of the first line, whilst in the direction of width its extent depends upon the unity of the work in hand, which again chiefly depends upon the nature of the ground.

It is always better to occupy the approaches to a position by independent bodies, and not to make such approaches boundaries between sections of the position.

The best formation for a battalion on the defensive, is generally that of separate company columns, whether, as a whole, it be formed in one or more lines.

6. The value and necessity of a second line of battle are much more evident for a defensive than for an attacking force; but its strength, and the manner in which it is drawn up and handled, depend entirely on the nature of the ground, according to which it will come into action either as an " inner " or " outer " reserve, for the latter of which offices a third *line of battle* will often become necessary when the numbers are large; and its operations will be conducted almost entirely on the principles of the offensive return (the more so, the larger the dimensions of the forces engaged), even when it does not of itself attempt to produce a decisive result.

Above all, an infusion of the offensive element should never be wanting to the *passive Defence* even in the smallest particulars.

7. It should be a principle of the *passive Defence* to open fire upon the enemy only when he comes within the most effective range.

All the same it will be necessary to take advantage of the extreme range of the arm by detaching small parties to fire, under the control of their officers, on the enemy's general line of approach, as far as it is known.

The first line will by a lively fire, and eventually

by *rapid independent firing*, keep the enemy's skirmishers at as great a distance as possible when they are taking up their ground previous to the assault, for the defence will be best served by their being hindered from establishing themselves firmly at this moment. Every fire-arm should be brought into play to the fullest extent against the actual assault at from 400 to 300 paces.

The defenders must be convinced that it may be necessary, after all, to have recourse to the bayonet, and that this would be less dangerous to them than to give way.

8. From the very nature of the work, a defensive action can only be carried through in *extended order*, to adopt which, from the very first, both supports and reserve may easily be forced.

Still, even with troops thus extended, the power of concentrating fire must be preserved, although it will rarely now be able to take the form of a volley.

The intermixture of skirmishers with supports will, for the *Defence* as for the *Attack*, be generally the only form of reinforcement possible, although exceptions to this rule may occur in the earlier stages of the fight, exceptions always to be made use of.

II. THE STAGE OF COUNTER-ATTACK.

The counter-attack of the Defensive-Offensive is its decisive act of offence. Hence it is not necessary here to speak of numbers, formations, or principles of execution, all which matters have been settled when treating of the *Offensive.*   It remains to us only in this place to clear up one point, but certainly the most material one for the counter-attack, namely, at what moment it should be made.

We have already pointed out as a fundamental condition of success in attack that the shock of the masses should follow immediately upon the preparatory operations.   The same condition holds good in the case of the counter-attack of the *Defensive-Offensive* force, if the defensive stage is really to be a preparation for it.

Success, on the whole, depends upon choosing the right moment for action.   This moment is self-evident in the case of the attack, which adheres simply to the same mode of fighting throughout, but for the *Defensive-Offensive* force which will deal its blow with other troops hitherto far away from the front, and therefore more fresh, the question of when ? and where ? so decisive for the attack, must be solved, and the answer acted upon as speedily as possible and under the most trying conditions.

The first thing, then, to be done is to fix upon the most favourable moment, and thereupon to settle upon the best position for the troops destined to make the movement.

The worst time for the assailant to exert his power of resistance is, doubtless, that at which he puts all his strength into offensive action.

Hence it follows, as a matter of course, that the most favourable moment for the counter-attack is that in which the assailant is advancing to the assault. If the *Defence* has done its duty, the attacking force is just then, whilst advancing without shelter and in a mass, as much shaken in respect of its power of resistance as it could ever expect the opposing force to be. Doubtless, its offensive power is, at such a moment, raised to its highest pitch, and this is more the consequence of human nature than of tactical rules; but this force and energy are only of avail in *one* direction, and that is *forwards.*

A counter-attack made at this moment on the flank has great, very great chance of success. All that has been remarked about the attack and its formation in *lines of battle* is in its favour.

To fall upon the flank of the assailant at the very moment that he makes his assault, must be the special aim of the Defender, as in this manner the counter-attack of the *Defensive-Offensive* is likely to be most telling. But when we consider the questions of time and space, and that, as we have seen, the assailant is to some extent prepared for the attempt, no one will deny that it is not quite an easy matter.

Before we proceed to inquire into the ways and means by which the *Defensive-Offensive* can arrive at this end, it will be advisable to determine whether there are not other moments favourable for the counter-stroke.

Let us examine, in the first place, the preceding stages of the combat.

A well-led attacking force advancing in a close, compact line, followed at a suitable distance by second and third lines of battle, will seldom or ever give the Defender the chance of making a successful counter-attack until the fire of the troops in position at the most telling range has shaken it. The only circumstances which will justify the Defender in assuming the offensive before he has made the most of his fire to give the enemy a warm reception, are faults in the dispositions made by the latter, or a gap in the advancing line occasioned by want of instruction on the part of his troops; in short, mere accidents. Even if in the course of the action it should appear likely that the effect produced by the fire would not be as great as was perhaps expected beforehand, as the defender promised to himself from his position (which in such a case must have been ill-chosen), it still remains more than doubtful whether a change of purpose, a relinquishment of the defensive for the offensive, would offer a better prospect than a consistent execution of the original plan, even if that were not absolutely the best which might have been adopted. It generally answers better in war to go through steadily with what you have determined on doing, than to fly off suddenly to some other scheme, even if you think that the latter might have answered better from the beginning. If, then, we have once accepted battle on the *Defensive-*

Offensive, let us carry it out, until a counter-attack has, at least comparatively, the best chance of success.

But the case is different when it is a question of taking advantage of manifest errors on the part of the assailant. An active Defender should not neglect such opportunities, but the counter stroke will then assume the character of a sortie, not that of a real change to decisively offensive action. Unless disorder, want of energy, and other faults have shown themselves un-mistakably on the part of the attacking force, it will never be advisable for the *Defensive-Offensive* force to sally forth directly from its position with the troops which had been told off for *passive Defence.*

And even for the partial sorties it will be advisable not to employ the troops actually holding the position, but only their "outer" reserves, particularly cavalry, and to recall them as soon as the short sally has had its effect.

The counter-attack, if made immediately after the assailant's final rush, does not at least suffer from not having waited for the effects of effective preparatory defensive-fire, as do premature sallies, such as above alluded to.

We pointed out in the previous chapter that an attacking force, even if successful, is not in a very fa-vourable condition for withstanding an attack, which consideration leads to making dispositions calculated to help the assailant through this period of weakness, but as in any case there is some difficulty in bringing the reinforcements (the third line of battle) into action at the right time, this moment will always be decidedly the most favourable for the defender's counter-stroke.

Whenever then it is not possible to fall with fresh troops upon the flank of the enemy just as he is advancing to the assault, this second opportunity will be used for the purpose.

According to old tactical rules, the flank attack was of universal application, because obstacles in front of the position generally hindered any movement in that direction.

From measures of this description arise those long-protracted struggles for localities which distinguished the Napoleonic wars, and which now, partly indeed for other reasons beside that above given, have become so much less frequent. The rule that the defender should charge the assailant when he gets within 30 paces on open ground is also based upon the same theory.

It cannot be denied that the front attack offers less chance of decisive success than the flank attack, because the latter has the unmistakable advantages first, of being executed on troops which have been more cut up beforehand; secondly, as the *passive Defence* co-operates to the last moment, of being able to bring larger forces into play; and lastly, of drawing at once the assailant's supporting troops, themselves the object of attack, into a partnership of loss with their advanced line, thus depriving the commander of the attack of the advantage of having his reserves at his disposal.

Having thus indicated the opportunities, or the opportunity for action, it now remains to make the best of them.

This problem, which to us appears the most difficult in the difficult art of command, resolves itself into the following question : In what part of the position should the troops intended to make the counter-attack be drawn up?

Unfortunately, the answer which we find so commonly given in manuals and essays as a complete solution, although it be undoubtedly accurate, is by no means exhaustive; this answer being that you should place the troops referred to under cover, where they will, as far as can be foreseen, be required, and near enough to come to the scratch at the right moment.

There are, doubtless, in all military operations, great and small, a vast number of questions which must be left to the judgment, acuteness, and genius of the commander to decide; but it is difficult to name a point upon which theory can give so little guidance as upon this particular one. We do not claim the merit of supplying this want. What we have above said about the most favourable moment for the counter-attack will show that we consider the most desirable post for the troops which are to make it, to be in rear of a flank of the position, thus at the same time any turning movement or flank attack being best provided against.

But under certain conditions the counter-stroke may also be dealt upon the enemy's *flank* from a position between two of the main points of occupation, and this is the object which we must try our utmost to attain.   But having said this, almost everything is exhausted which we can contribute to the subject, and we conclude with no other answer but that it depends upon circumstances whether we place the troops in question behind one or both wings, whether we place them in the centre eventually or at first,—how near to the front line, &c., &c.*

But because this *was* so, and *is* so, and because it must surely be granted that the officer who, acting "according to circumstances," hits upon the very best course, is a somewhat rare creature, therefore we said above : the change of form of action necessary for the counter-stroke, makes the *Defensive-Offensive* so remarkably difficult, and everything connected with it is so dependent on "circumstances," that we must reject it as a form of action to be recommended on principle. We will not deny or fail to recognize that in *theory* the attractions of the *Defensive-Offensive* as a tactical principle in many ways surpass those of the pure *Offensive ;* but when you come to *practice,* so many "if's" and "but's" come into play, that but little of the fascination remains.

It is not too much to say that only a general with the

---

* These "circumstances" themselves usually depend upon the choice of a position, and upon its *offensive capabilities,* subjects which do not now concern us.

most perfect eye, and troops the most thoroughly capable of manœuvering appear fit to undergo this ordeal.

Only once did even a *Napoleon* carry out this change of form in the middle of a battle, and that was at Austerlitz ; the number of instances, however, in which even a so-called victorious *Defensive* army has been stopped by the difficulties of the second part of its task, so that the battle in consequence remained undecided, almost equals the number of the defensive battles themselves.[*]

All that we have said remains unaltered by the fact that our battles and combats of the present day fought with arms and masses of men unheard of since the invention of gunpowder, will lead more often than formerly to a comparatively indecisive measuring of strength, more seldom than formerly to a victory which really annihilates the enemy, because both daylight and strength must fail before the way can be properly prepared for the decisive onslaught, and because both sides remain too much exhausted to begin again next day. And the cases which will be of more frequent occurrence now than formerly, of masses being compelled to fight entirely on the *Defensive*, without any hope of gaining a *real* victory, but simply with the intention of maintaining themselves in the position which they have taken up, will make no alteration in these principles.

---

[*] Some of Wellington's battles may be quoted as successful instances of the *Defensive-Offensive*; notably Salamanca, where the "second part of the task" was well performed. — (Tr.)

(Such combats may be called *covering* actions, for instance against sorties or attempts at relief.)

We must, however, always strive for a decisive result, and the only unalterable task of theory is to point out the way to arrive at such.

But if, as a deduction from this, it should be asserted that in future all combats will assume the form of action in which both parties take the *Offensive*, this must to a certain extent be allowed.* Battles in which both sides take the *Offensive* (Rencontreschlacht), and the attack and defence of fortresses and entrenched camps were the only forms of warfare before powder came as an agent so completely in favour of the Defence, which character it no longer continues to retain.

But if, speaking generally, victory should be the object of every battle, it is evident how extremely important it must be to deprive the enemy of his initiative for attack.

Thus, the study of the *Defensive-Offensive* brings us back at last to the purest *Offensive*.

The principles which present themselves to us as a consequence of this study of the second stage of the Defensive-Offensive are pretty much as follows :

1. The *Defensive-Offensive* must carefully separate the troops intended for the two purposes of Defence and Counter-attack; allotting to the former as far as possible a minimum of force, if the position be favourable.

---

* Reasons for assuming the *Defensive* are given above, and what has been said of its consequences is not without a weakening tendency.

2. The strong main-body is intended to deal the counter-stroke best of all on the enemy's flank just as he is advancing to storm the position; otherwise, at least as soon as possible after the assailant has actually forced his way in; only as an exceptional case, when the assailant makes gross mistakes or shows timidity, should the counter-attack be made before the fire of the Defence has had its full effect.

3. The counter-attack as an act of offence is governed entirely, both as to form and execution, by the same principles which regulate the attack, that is to say, it should be quick, concentrated, and energetic.

4. The position chosen for the body of troops intended to make the counter-attack, is one of the most difficult as well as one of the most important problems which a commander has to solve. Being entirely dependent on circumstances for time and place, the offensive return can only produce a decisive result if made at the right moment. This consideration must guide the commander in selecting a position, and also in deciding upon the further dispositions and orders which are certain to be required. The only principle which can be laid down is to keep the troops concealed under cover, if possible behind a flank.

5. The combination of defence and counter-attack, and the necessary transition from one to the other are of such direct and decisive consequence to the *Defensive-Offensive*, that this form of action is only to be re-

commended if the commander be thoroughly competent and the troops extremely fit to manœuvre.

III. SOME REMARKS ON DRILL.

All that we have since said on the Defence has not
in the least affected the assertion made in our chapter
on the Offensive, that extended order had become practically the only fighting formation for infantry. We
find the line of skirmishers, the swarm of skirmishers
as much in the *Defence* as in the *Attack*, nay, even
more generally and imperatively required in the former
than in the latter ; and in the former also more than in
the latter, the company column comes into the foreground as the actual foundation of skirmishing order.
It must be admitted that in the *Defence* the company is,
almost without exception, to be regarded as the tactical
unit, whilst in the *Attack* this cannot everywhere be
allowed. All the deductions, then, in respect of drill
formations which were drawn from these premises at
the conclusion of the second chapter would here have
simply to be repeated ; but we may mention that the
requirements of the *Defence* furnish further arguments
in favour of the three-deep formation, and of the subdivision of the company into four parts resulting
from it.

It would be hardly necessary to revert again to
the drill regulations, were we not bound to say a few
words upon a subject so intimately connected with the

Defence which is based upon the action of firearms, as the volley, a form of fire which has been warmly recommended for defensive purposes.

The extraordinary effect, particularly on the *morale* which the sudden discharge of a great shower of bullets at the same moment is apt to produce upon an enemy under certain conditions, is assuredly not undervalued by us, laying stress, as we often have done, upon the effects of even unaimed fire.

On the contrary, and just because we so much value this powerful agent, we desire for the troops which have to make use of it, the adoption of a formation which will expose them less than that of compact close order, the only one hitherto imagined for this purpose, to the especially severe losses which may be expected at those *particular* moments. It will, in future, be almost impossible to bring up to the front, or to direct lines in close order at such moments as demand the volley, and indeed this has already been proved, except in the case of quite small detachments under peculiarly favourable conditions. As a means of training we may, and indeed we should continue to practise this old-established form, but we can only employ the volley in action, when feasible, from extended order by signal. A shrill whistle of the leader of the line or swarm of skirmishers, of the clump or group, gives, as far as it can be heard, the signal to make "ready," or, as the case may be, to "cease firing," even when *rapid independent firing* is going on ; the whistle repeated after

L

that for the "ready" is the signal to "commence firing," which every soldier must at once obey, at least every one who can fire without hurting his neighbour. This requires drill.

There is nothing new in this at bottom, but it is well that it should become matter of regulation.

Lastly, the question of the *square* belongs also to the domain of *Defence.* From all we have been saying about the fighting formation for infantry, it cannot be doubted that we consider the square an impossibility as long as the enemy's guns and rifles are within effective range. The smaller detachments will sometimes have to form " clumps," but the battalion square can only now be used when hostile cavalry masses come on without the support of the other arms ; certainly a rare, if not an impossible case.

One more remark may be here permitted, although it does not actually concern infantry field-exercise. In treating both of *Offensive* and of *Defensive-Offensive,* we have dwelt much less than was thought formerly necessary, particularly in the early days of the breech-loader, upon the importance of avoiding the so-called "waste of ammunition."

In fact, it is one of the most important advantages of the breech-loader, that it *can* fire away a great quantity of ammunition, and war experience has taught us that, far differently to what was in other days the case, we must now take count of chance hits and unaimed shots.

The arm is equal to the task, the frequently momentous results of its fire are well-established ; it remains to supply the ammunition.

Constant and plentiful relays of ammunition are a necessity of life for infantry now-a-days, which necessity must be supplied. We must not omit all notice of this point in these remarks on drill, although it does not strictly belong to our subject. Besides the circumstance that the relation between gun and ammunition waggon is a subject of artillery-regulation, may also serve to show that the above observation is not out of place.

CHAPTER IV.

In the first chapter of this study, we pointed out the difference between fighting which aims at a decisive result and that which does not do so, whilst in the two succeeding chapters we gave a sufficient illustration of the decisive forms of action, as far as general principles are concerned, so that we think we may here dispense with further argument.

It is indeed difficult to imagine a more striking contrast than exists between those endeavours to annihilate the enemy based upon the most extreme energy in offence, or upon the most stubborn tenacity in defence, and the objects aimed at in the action with which we now have to deal, namely, to gain time, or to occupy, perhaps to hold a certain point, if possible without fighting.

In our chapters on the *Offensive* and on the *Defensive-Offensive*, we alluded to the necessity of an "introductory" phase of action, as enabling the commander to come to a right decision as to the course to be pursued ; in the period preceding this "introductory" stage, reconnoissances will be required which will usually bring those making them into collision with the enemy's out-posts. The commander who wishes to avoid a decisive operation, or to escape if possible the consequences of one which has turned out badly, can only do so by means of a rear-guard; and so on.

· All detachments intended for these "introductory," "reconnoitring," "outpost," or "rear-guard," purposes, in fact, all troops meant to carry on " la petite guerre," act so far in the same manner that they neither desire to, can, or ought to bring things to the crisis of destroying or being destroyed (at any rate this may always be said of one side).

Nevertheless, as in war, the fact of our opponent not wishing a thing to happen is sufficient reason for the other to desire it, these tasks will very rarely be performed except by force of arms. And after all, a decisive result lies at the root of all military action.

To escape from this dilemma, requires, it must be confessed, a different mode of handling troops than does the clear and precise aiming at an actual result. If we search for the characteristics common to all action of this kind, for the means by which, according to both practice and theory, this difficult task of avoiding battle, at least by one side, is to be accomplished, we shall find that all bodies of troops thus employed will always make a show of adopting either the *Offensive* or the *Defensive* form of action, so as, by threatening the enemy with it, to deceive, mislead, and induce him to take false steps.

The advanced-guard of an attacking force, which is leading the way with the view of making out the details of the hostile position, will be compelled, in order to settle upon the principal line of attack, to make at once a show of being really the attacking force, for the purpose of misleading the enemy, and of tempting him to unmask his strength early.

So also the outposts, or the rear-guard of the Defensive force, in retiring upon the main position must here and there make a show of intending to offer decided resistance, so as to induce the assailant, if possible, to make a premature deployment, and to draw him after them in the desired direction. Reconnoissances will often by false attacks, distract the enemy's attention from the point which is really of importance. Rear-guards are very difficult to handle, because they cannot always maintain the imposing attitude required of them for the purpose of forcing the enemy to make turning movements, or of delaying him in some other way.

We may describe, in a few words, this sort of fight to be something which appears different to what it is, and which tries to be thought something different.

Feint, deceit, allurement, demonstration, are the life-elements of this style of conflict, for which perhaps the *Demonstrative*, will be a more suitable comprehensive expression, than the *temporising Combat*.

But as now the power of Striking and that of Resisting are the only two strings of the instrument (the armed force), and as the *Offensive* and the *Defensive* are the only two notes of its music (Tactics) which are produced by these strings, nothing remains to the *Demonstrative* but to use these notes in happy alternation.

Having seen that the *Offensive* cannot exist without an infusion of the *Defensive*, nor the *Defensive* without some intermixture of the *Offensive*, it will now be recognised as the task of the *Demonstrative* to act sometimes offensively, at others defensively, so as to make the most of both the primary forms of action by the most judicious combination possible ; in other words, to manœuvre skilfully.

In order to be equal to this task, the fighting formation must needs be of a very flexible, mobile character, —a formation which will accommodate itself easily, and without friction to all circumstances, taking advantage of these if favourable, and if not so evading the danger.

The Feint, with pliability soft as wax, requires very different combinations to the *struggle for life and death*, with method hard and unyielding as iron.

On the part of the soldier mobility, on the part of the officer, from highest to lowest, readiness to act on his own responsibility and decision, are qualities indispensable to success in these operations. Although we only wish here to speak particularly of Infantry, and the other arms do not concern us, this seems the place to mention that all these tasks are specially suited to well-armed Cavalry and Horse Artillery, which have again, in the last wars, played so prominent a part as *advanced-* and *rear-guard*. May they then no longer stick at the *word*; the *thing* itself is of the very greatest importance, and its performance affords the most brilliant opportunities to genius, aptitude for war, and fitness for command.[*]

But let us return to the Infantry. The two fundamental requirements noticed as affecting the question of formation, leave no room for doubt that Infantry can only meet them by using the company column.

This formation is the basis of skirmishing, and only the action of skirmishers carried to its fullest extent can perform for Infantry what the *Demonstrative* requires. Any order more or less *close*, of itself leads to decisive action, which extended order alone gives the power to avoid, and at the same time to threaten.

We here contrast *close* and *extended* order with reference to the employment of individual portions of the battle array, not as above, when in contrasting mass and individual formations we referred to the employment of the individual man.

In this sense, we say, *extended order* alone can be employed successfully in the *Demonstrative*, viewing it as the exact opposite to *close order* as required, speaking generally, in the *Offensive* and *Defensive-Offensive*; extended order alone enables us to evacuate a defensive position without incurring a defeat; it alone

---

[*] In this Infantry-study there can be no question of the employment of Cavalry in battle.

admits of an attacking movement without being exposed to the evils of a repulse.

This first main requirement of the *Demonstrative* will have the further consequence, that in all such combats troops must be spread out over a broader front than with the two main forms of action, each of which in its way, sets so high a value upon concentration.

The object of all these engagements is, according to circumstances, to gain a sight of the enemy or to hinder him from seeing you. Both objects, however, always require a certain extension of front, but may almost and entirely dispense with depth of formation, because the *Demonstrative* force nowhere wishes to be a prime agent, and at the same time the main body, the great mass of the host of which it is only a fraction, is coming up behind it.

Still, the greater the numbers the less will it be able to dispense entirely with some sort of reserve. But when compared with the *decisive* forms of action, the *Demonstrative* will only present the mere image of a *first line*, and of a *reserve* held back to meet a case of extremity.

The more this tendency to extension of front makes itself felt, the more difficult unity of command will of course become, the more capable of independent action must be the fractions which stand side by side. The Commanding Officer's task can therefore only be specified in a very general manner ; it cannot, as in the cases

of *Attack* and *Defence*, be distinctly determined by having a special point assigned to take or to hold ; again,
subordinate officers will not have, as in those cases,
their allotted parts to play, but only general directions,
and this rule will probably hold good down to the
lowest grades, each individual perhaps getting the
chance of solving the whole problem by himself.

A patrol which reaches the favourable point from
whence the hostile position can be surveyed, a picket
which hinders a mischievous reconnoissance, a weak
detachment in advance of a defensive position, or in a
rear-guard action which compels the opponent's force to
deploy, has done all that could be expected of it, and it
will be able to do this under certain circumstances, for
the object to be attained is not so much to win the
fight itself, as to gain time or some local advantage.

Even if the one detachment which accomplishes this
be destroyed, all the other troops at hand merely de-
monstrating, the task will yet have been executed.

Would this be possible except by using totally different formations and dispositions to those applicable to
the great decisive battles of the masses ?

Having established as the most judicious form of
action that of a line of independent company columns
with greater or smaller intervals, each company further-
ing the common object to the best of its ability, the indirect manner in which they will co-operate will explain
itself. These small bodies fighting side by side will
each be too weak either of itself to make directly a real

attack or a serious resistance, but they will play into one another's hands by mutual action on the flanks. Each will send forth its skirmishers, opening a very heavy fire wherever the enemy shows himself in force, but quickly avoiding his attack, to try the same game anew at another place if he assumes the offensive, or tries to hold his opponent fast by an obstinate resistance.

These partial engagements take the place of that unity of action which is only found in carrying out the general plan of operations ; hence, however, the risk of partial defeats.

However damaging such a check may be to the particular enterprise in hand, it is but of secondary importance in itself, and only becomes dangerous when the commander in rear gives way to the temptation of trying to extricate a detachment thus compromised, and in this manner is very likely to become involved in a serious engagement against his own will, and contrary to the general object of his operations, which should always be kept clearly in view.*

It may seem a hard thing to say, but still it should be established as a principle, that the captains to whom belongs the honour of these fights, must undertake

---

* At Spicheren, Wörth, and Borny, the German commanders became involved in serious engagements against their own will, in consequence of the initiative taken by the leaders of their advanced guards. In each case they supported the detachment compromised, and the result was most satisfactory, because the action of the advanced guards, though in two cases, at least, premature, was on the whole consistent with the general object of the operations. —(Tr.)

them at their own risk and on their own responsibility.

They will get support from the neighbouring companies in line with them, but must not reckon upon any from the rear.

It stands to reason that we do not mean to imply that it should be an absolute and imperative rule that on no account is one company to be kept back behind another, that all must be scattered into one long line of skirmishers, and so forth. We have only meant to treat the question in the abstract, and all that should be deduced from what we have said amounts simply to this : the *Demonstrative* neither knows nor ought to know either the recklessness of the *Attack à outrance*, which is ready to venture all, or the tenacity of the obstinate *Defence* which is prepared to sacrifice all.

The *Demonstrative* will have to vary and modify its action in a hundred different ways according to its special task, to its absolute and relative strength, to the nature of the ground, and to the enemy's measures, for which reason we name a flexible formation as that best suited to it. And so we sum up as follows :—

1. Every body of troops engaged in decisive operations requires to have a number of secondary tasks executed beyond their scope, and both before and after them. Such tasks are rarely to be performed except by force of arms, yet have but little to do with the final object of every real battle, namely, decisive victory.

All these reconnoitring, outpost, advanced, and rear-guard actions may be comprehended in the term *Demonstrative combats.*

2. It is to the interest of every force intended for decisive action to employ only as few troops as possible, and only the infantry absolutely necessary to gain the object in view.

3. These troops will sometimes act offensively, at other times defensively, but as they never aim at a decisive result, and as their task is always rather to gain time and room, they never make a real attack or a real defence.

4. To perform the work required of them their formation should be very flexible, and with more front than depth, only consisting of one line, with maybe a reserve held back. The line of company columns with skirmishers will be the best formation for the purpose.

5. With this looseness of formation the chief Commander can only give general directions to the different independent fractions, and eventually come up to their support. The result will depend more than in any other situation upon the subordinate officers ; indeed, at times, it may be brought about by any one of them.

6. The operation will always, on the whole, be only an indirect one, for all direct action involves the danger, against which there is and can be no remedy of leading to the undesired crisis. Success will depend solely on

the skill with which detachments acting side by side play into each other's hands.

So much for principles; one word more to conclude :—

When we first in this study explained the difference between combats aiming at a decisive result and those not doing so, we pointed out the great importance of drawing the same distinction in the general principles of instruction for our infantry, and we think that a nearer consideration of the various formations has served to prove the correctness of our views.

The *Demonstrative* requires nothing in the way of drill in addition to what was noted for the two main forms of action, it simply ratifies their wants in this respect. But if we only picture to ourselves superficially (and our treatment of the subject in this place can only be superficial, as we cannot here enlarge upon the training of our troops), the demands which each of these modes of fighting makes upon our infantry, we must confess that they necessarily vary according to the object in view.

But we are inclined to think that the smaller objects are more attended to in our peace-instruction than are the greater.

Must that not, or at least may that not easily lead to seeking great results where only small ones are to be found ?

In other words, may not our *Field-exercise* spoil our *Fighting ?*

The bold and vigorous features of the *Offensive*

and *Defensive-Offensive* present a strong contrast to the delicately shaded outline of the *Demonstrative.*

From the private to the captain, careful instruction in details is the chief thing for all ranks; that is to say, they should be made good shots, be educated to a thorough knowledge of how to take advantage of the ground, and to a complete mastery of every tactical formation, also to quick perception; this training will culminate in the battalion-commander's capacity for handling his companies, and all this preliminary instruction will have its good effect further on; after this comes the training of masses from the battalion up to the division.

Now, in our army, there is no want of guidance, zeal, or in general of intelligence in carrying out the first part of this course, and far be it from us to detract in any way from the merit of our soldiers ; but for the last part of the course, what we urgently want above all is more time.

The battalions of a regiment are assembled yearly for a few days on the drill-ground, which may do, and the regiments of a brigade are scrambled together somehow (yet they, too, should learn how to manœuvre).

But the division, the battle-unit, is assembled barely once or twice a year. The manœuvres as a rule represent only fighting in extended order, not the action of the masses at the critical moment.

And yet is it not wonderfully difficult to know how

to bring the masses into play at the right time : to deploy masses here and there when needed ; to combine the movements of the masses ; in one word, to direct the masses ?

May we be able to find time and opportunity for these lessons, lest war should have to teach us what we ought already to have learnt in peace, what like is *Battle ! ! !*

PART II.

THE PEACE SCHOOL.

(PREPARATION FOR WAR IN PEACE).

INTRODUCTION.

WHEN we endeavoured in the first part of these studies to find an answer to the question, what alterations in the Tactics of Infantry have been forced upon us by the introduction of the improved arms now in use, our attention was repeatedly drawn to the degree of tactical success which may be attained in war by having previously, during peace, made ourselves familiar with the necessary formations.

" The school of peace (war-training in time of peace) can alone enable us to overcome the enormous friction of the battle-field;" this is what we then at once recognized as a fact; hence the following question would only appear to be the natural sequel to the enquiry then commenced,—what effect will its results, with reference to formations suitable to war, be calculated to produce in matter and manner, upon the training of our infantry during peace? It must at once be admitted that the new order of things has raised to no inconsiderable extent the demands which must be made as well upon the soldier individually as upon a body of troops collectively and upon its leaders up to the very highest grade.

Extended order, which is acknowledged to be now the only possible fighting formation, requires higher qualities than were ever before expected in the private soldier; the extension of the sphere of danger renders it necessary for a body of troops to be more capable of manœuvring than ever; the increased complication of command in battle, together with the more than heretofore irrevocable nature of its results, require on the part of the leaders a well-trained tactical judgment, all the more that they have both to deal much oftener with elements strange to them, and always to operate with much greater masses, than in other days.

Now although there is nothing positively new either in the formations alluded to or in the educational requirements based upon them, nevertheless the influence, the value, the importance of such training compared to what was given in former days, are as much raised on the whole as they are modified in matters of detail. And doubtless, if our army wishes to maintain the pre-eminence now attained in face of future foes, it must necessarily devote its constant attention to this continual process of change, for which reason a more complete enquiry into the question is justified.

The most complete self-reliance on the part of the individual soldier, the greatest power of manœuvring on that of the troops, combined with a good military eye on the part of subordinate officers, and with thorough capacity for directing the masses on the part of those in higher command; these are the qualities which in the main form the groundwork for that successful unity of action which leads to victory.

To prepare beforehand all these elements of success is the task, and by no means a light one, of our peace-training, a task, however difficult, which must be accomplished if an army is to be fitted to its work. Now the instruction of the individual soldier in detail has been already for many years a fundamental principle of our method of training during peace; the practical field-manœuvres of our army enjoy an European renown; the theoretical preparatory teaching of our officers is avowedly of a high standard; upon all which the results of three campaigns have impressed the stamp of actual proof.

With such facts before us we may be justified in maintaining that the fundamental principles of our peace-training should continue stedfast and immovable, whilst only such modifications should be made as experience has shown to be necessary. Above all let us be careful not to meddle with any part of what our peace school has so pre-eminently contributed towards

the creation of discipline, of patriotism, of the love of
honour, in short to the moral phase of military
education.

We, who have here only to do with tactical training, are
simply called upon to enquire how far what has hitherto
been aimed at, and accomplished, in this way during
peace, has approved itself in war, and consequently
what improvements may be made therein. For, however great may be the pleasure with which we look
back to the success obtained, a careful examination of
our tactics will reveal much to the impartial eye of the
critic which might well have been different. And we
cannot be surprised that such was and is the case when
we consider that the colossal technical alterations which
the present age has brought forth were tried for the
first time practically against one another in the war of
1870-71, and that it would have been more than rash to
throw over a well-tried system of peace-training on
account of mere theoretical speculations.

Now, however, we are in a position to estimate by
means of the scale of experience the length and breadth
of the edifice which it is necessary to erect. But
measuring by this scale what has been already accomplished and what remains to be done, we cannot but
admit that, however complete and sufficient the training
of our soldiers, non-commissioned officers, and subalterns
has proved itself to be, as far as the sphere of operations of each individual extends, they have often, very
often been wanting in a clear and comprehensive in-

telligence 'of how to co-operate for a common end ; moreover, however well acquainted our captains, field officers, and generals have shown themselves with the requirements of war generally and with the conduct of troops in action particularly, they have met with great, often insurmountable difficulties in making their respective commands fit into the great battle-frame as parts of one and the same picture.

Making therefore all due acknowledgment of what was accomplished in detail, we cannot avoid confessing that the tactical errors of our infantry were numerous, very numerous, and more especially so where things were on a larger scale, which errors may entirely be laid to the charge of a system of instruction in peace which fails to meet the requirements of modern battle, requirements which, to be sure, have only quite lately made themselves felt.

To what other cause but to insufficient familiarity with and *practice* in such matters, for *theories* have never been wanting, can the following effects be attributed ; that we so often saw our Infantry rush headlong to the charge without giving our Artillery sufficient time or opportunity to prepare the way ; that great bodies of troops trickled away into action before completing their march into line of battle ; that detachments standing or fighting side by side made their attacks independently of one another instead of in combination ; that comparatively weak bodies (advanced guards, for instance) assumed an extension of front far more than commensurate with their strength, and that separate battalions, companies, even at last divisions, breaking away here and there from their " stem," and seeking each its own way, doubled in, attacked, made turning movements, pursued, each "on its own hook," until utterly breathless, and with ammunition expended, they found themselves at the opposite end of the battle-field. And how many more such examples might be given !

We must freely admit that faults of this sort became less frequent as the war went on, that our Infantry acquired on the battle-fields the routine in which it had been at first in this respect deficient ; but it appears to us that this very fact should all the more induce us to regulate our work in peace in such a manner that such-like improvements should no longer remain to be made in war, and that the "peace-school" of the future may steer clear of error as it may do, if it takes for its guide the well-considered lessons of the late war, fruitful as they are of instruction, and conclusive, at any rate, for the immediate future.

But let us not flatter ourselves with the hope that the war-experience just gained will alone be sufficient to fulfil this object. Even if it were kept longer in view than is avowedly the case during the "piping times of peace," the value of its lessons is often very problematical unless sifted and regulated by criticism.

Final deductions from " personal experiences " often

take a wonderfully false twist. For instance, we saw how after 1866 a man, with an otherwise clear and observing mind, and one which extracted much that was true, went so far in his " Retrospect " as to assert, with many believers, that the right course for infantry to follow was to fight in future "like a horde of savages ! "

If just now at least, when recent events are still fresh in our memory, such a doctrine will no longer find many disciples, and the elimination, on principle, of all superior direction will hardly at this moment be a maxim of even the most fanatical theorist, it is advisable nevertheless to oppose to it a firmer barrier than that of mere " individual war-experience." There is only one sure way of preserving ourselves in future from a relapse into such erroneous doctrine, the facile offspring of " personal experiences," and that way is to have *fixed precepts founded upon the wants of war.*

Let us then sum up the objects we are aiming at :—

The foundation of our peace-school has approved itself throughout, but the building which we have at once to erect upon this base must be calculated to render the same service to the altered tactics of the present day as was rendered by the old edifice to those of an earlier period.

In other words, battle *as it is now* must again be the principal object of our peace-training, just as battle, *as it was then,* used to be the principal object of our training in former days. Again, to be in keeping with the phraseology of the first part of these studies, we will say :—

Our peace-instruction should make a more radical distinction than has been done hitherto between the *Decisive* and the *Demonstrative* * forms of action.

We do not conceal from ourselves that great, but we think not insurmountable, difficulties stand in the way of this modern "labour of peace." If we shall always find much which bears upon such work to be totally unrepresentable in peace; if first and foremost the necessity of more costly and more frequent gatherings of great masses of troops must be accepted, there will yet be much, very much to be done in the way of preparation in the earlier and even in the earliest stages of our instruction in addition to those "great reviews" of the great Frederick which seem to have been revived.

And to that army which gained such great successes on the battle-fields of the late war by its invincible spirit, and by pouring forth its best heart's blood, the faculty will hardly be denied of raising in peace time its new tactics to the level of its well-proved strategy, and of assigning to the art of fighting battles the place which it ought to hold amongst the other qualities which that army so eminently possesses. If we keep the object aimed at in view, to make progress

* The *skirmishing-tactics* which originated in 1870—71 differ as much from the *column-tactics* of Napoleon, as these differed from the *line-tactics* of Frederick ; it remains for us to develop the new system as far as the strength of man will admit.

with the training of the soldier both individually and collectively, and then with the higher instruction of the officers, we shall perhaps succeed, by making desirable modifications and improvements in these respects, in working up beforehand for the great field-manœuvres a material by means of which these representations of war will make as near an approach to reality as can possibly be attained in peace.

CHAPTER I.

THE TRAINING OF SOLDIERS INDIVIDUALLY AND COLLECTIVELY.

In face of modern requirements it is no longer allowable to follow the old custom of fixing upon a *certain proportion of matter* the infusion of which would convert a man into a perfect soldier.

Mechanical proficiency in externals, formerly of such primary importance, has lost its value in the same proportion as the soldier has ceased to be merely a wheel in the great military machine, and even where, as for instance in the use of the rifle, greater mechanical proficiency than ever is required of him, yet after all it is the independent and judicious use of the art of shooting by each individual which is the pith of the whole thing. The amount of actual matter which is drilled into a soldier no longer forms the only, hardly indeed even the main criterion of efficiency, which has come to depend much more upon his moral and intellectual qualities.

It will be hard to find anyone now who will be inclined to assign positive limits to the amount of what a soldier should know and be able to do, after which his military education may be considered complete, for the flexibility of modern tactics makes such an estimate of proficiency simply impossible. Hence it is evident, and was indeed evident before our last experiences, that with a system of short service during peace, and viewing the question of training simply from the point of view of a soldier, we are dealing, and can only deal with a relative minimum of instruction with which we must needs be satisfied ; on the other hand, also, that with the existing terms of service the instructor must endeavour to attain as far as possible at each moment of progressive development a certain relatively service-able degree of efficiency which would render his men at any time immediately fit for use.

In order to gain a clearer view of this point without at present going into the question of the means to be employed in military training—its *substance* and the final *result*—let us place before ourselves an ideal to be attained by it in working up a certain specified material.

To bring the man as individual combatant, and the individuals as joint combatants, to the highest possible pitch of warlike efficiency (fighting-capacity), to make soldiers of them, and of these soldiers to form organized bodies, such are the *material* objects of military *training ;* to raise both the individual and the body of men at the same time to the moral level of their task, is the aim of military *education*—an aim to be pursued from the very first, and to be regarded as on a par with the objects above mentioned.

So much for our aim ; now as regards the material out of which so much that is great and difficult has to be fashioned. This presents itself to us, as seen and judged from the technical standpoint, in the shape of a raw, *i.e.* totally unprepared mass.

Without its being here necessary for us to enter into historical dissertation and argument, it will doubtless be admitted that modern armies have, and must have, for their foundation the " mass-levy " of the nation, of which the great majority have up to the time of enrolment been entirely strange to the use of arms. Whilst in former days one was required only to form a limited number of professional soldiers, we are now called upon, under present conditions, both directly and indirectly more difficult, to train the mass of the people during a short period of service, to a higher standard of efficiency for war.

In face of such circumstances, the above-mentioned necessity of being " satisfied with a minimum " has already been long forced upon us ; but it becomes still more imperative when we compare actual circumstances with those of the time just passed. The demands upon us, as we have already pointed out in our introduction, have once more been increased ; the time allotted for meeting them remains the same. In deciding upon our future system of peace-training, we cannot help recognizing the greatest possible reduction in the quantity of things taught, if we do not wish to expose ourselves to a reduction of *quality* still more prejudicial. It is therefore necessary to enquire how far such reduction in *amount of matter* in favour of the maintenance and, wherever possible, of the elevation of the standard of *quality*, may and ought to go ; also whether, and if so, how this end may be promoted by the system of training. The further consideration of this important question will lead us soon to a distinction hitherto perhaps not fully appreciated between the warlike efficiency of soldiers as individuals and as a body.

For instance, it is not necessary, and, as one may suppose, has never been necessary, because never obtainable, that, for a body of troops to possess a general fitness for war, each member should be equally prepared to perform each one of the warlike tasks which that body may be called upon to accomplish.

If even it must be admitted in *theory* that a force composed only of perfectly-trained soldiers will produce the most perfect results, yet this commonplace is entirely worthless in *practice*, because based upon a mere Utopia of the present day. With things as they actually are, the question presents itself to us substantially in this wise ; Which body of troops is most fit for war, one composed of soldiers who have undergone a certain equal average degree of preparatory training for all the possible requirements of war, or one the majority of whose members are prepared to

perform with sufficient sureness the principal and
constantly-recurring tasks which devolve upon soldiers
in the field, whilst only a smaller number are initiated
in the more difficult and rarer operations of an indecisive character required on actual service ?

That nowadays we have only these two alternatives
before us, that it is practically impossible in the two or
three years at our disposal for training our men to
impart to every infantry soldier a sufficient degree of
efficiency in every possible situation of war, will, we
think, be admitted without further proof.

That man who only knows the outward forms and
manipulations of which he is to make use "under
certain circumstances," is not a proficient in his calling
or handicraft, but only he who thoroughly understands
their employment, and therefore knows for certain and
without doubt what he has to do in each individual
case.

But if a "peace-school," limited as to time, endeavours
on principle to train *every* soldier in *every* way as far as
time and circumstances allow, it is evident that such a
course must interfere with the higher instruction of
those who are gifted with more aptitude or taste for
the business than the less favourably endowed
majority, and that in consequence thereof only a
certain average efficiency can naturally be obtained as
the general result. If then, as is always the case,
certain individuals stand above the common level, they
will hardly surpass by their achievements the many

who remain below that level, so far that on the whole there should be a balance of gain. But the state of things will be very different, and certainly more favourable, if, taking count of individual aptitude in our peace-training, we aim at attaining for the body of troops collectively only what is absolutely necessary in war, and proceed to the more difficult tasks exclusively with those who have manifested real military aptitude, and these latter we shall have the power of educating to a much higher standard than heretofore, or without this classification ; whilst we shall gain time and opportunity to prepare the remainder, constituting the great majority, all the more thoroughly for their necessary labours. If then at any time any unusual task devolves upon a corps, the influence and example of the men who have been more thoroughly instructed with a view to the particular emergency, will act upon the rest ; so that the general efficiency aimed at will rather be increased than diminished. Our argument, then, may be summed up as follows : Whilst hitherto the edifice of our " peace-school " has been based upon the idea of aiming at imparting to each infantry soldier complete instruction, or at any rate instruction as varied as possible, so that the general standard should be raised by the sum of individual acquirements, we must now endeavour to erect a system of classification upon the undisturbed foundation of our old traditions.

And to do this nothing fundamentally new is re-

quired; this system of voluntary restriction to a certain
field of instruction has long been embodied with the
best results in our well-proved course of musketry
instruction; the evident practical utility of forming an
" upper class "* has already long since accustomed the
masses to this distinction in all the different branches;
but nevertheless it will neither be unadvisable or of
little importance to proclaim this doctrine clearly as the
leading principle of our method of instruction, so that
there should be perfect certainty as to our object.
Only by doing this will it be possible to knock the too
idealistic principle of universal perfection on the head,
a principle which endangers our success by its experi-
mental *tours de force*.   There can be no doubt that
the course we have pursued hitherto has been governed
by a longing for this " all-sidedness," as every possible
formation imaginable, every phase of combat has been
shown to the young soldier on the drill ground and at
field exercise from his very first year of service, the
practice of the following years being devoted to per-
fecting him in these lessons by repetition.   But if, in
face of the constantly increasing claims upon us, we
must once for all give up the hope of attaining this end
with *all* our men, an intentional and well-considered
system of *restriction* must incontestably be preferred to
trying how far we can possibly get   That such an
endeavour, if it does not really reach the acme, must
rather operate prejudicially than otherwise, manifests

* " Ausbildend," *i.e.*, improving, receiving cultivation.—Tn.

itself perhaps most clearly by the example of the course of development given to our peace-practice in fighting in extended order.

All our instructions, directions, and rules for guidance in this branch of our duties date from a time when the first commencement of a better armament, especially for our own troops, imparted an increased importance to the action of skirmishers in battle, although it still remained very far indeed from being estimated on a par with the action of the masses in close order. The situations of combat to which we have applied the common term "demonstrative," were naturally the only ones which could then be kept in view as objects of all our instruction in skirmishing. The highest possible development of the sharpshooter in this way passed as over and above sufficient for the secondary part which he had to play in the decisive engagements of columns. The *drill-ground*, with its double columns on the centre and skirmishers in the intervals, was our preparatory school for the conflict of masses, in other words for battle : our *field-exercise** served to train light infantry for their secondary tasks.

The short campaign of 1866 against the muzzle-loader had only immaterially disturbed these customary conditions of peace when the next war came with totally different demands on the army.

* "Felddienstübung," literally "Fieldservice-practice," which means a great deal more in Germany than what we in England understand by " Field-exercise," and for which we have hitherto had no fair equivalent either in word or deed.—Tr.

It cannot create surprise that, when the destructive effects of the latest inventions placed before the eyes of every individual the imperative necessity of breaking with all our old battle-traditions, our leaders of high and low degree, realising with quick determination the only possible change, substituted " field-exercise " for the evolutions of the drill-ground.

But battle in its present form is by no means field-exercise magnified.

The use of masses in extended order for *decisive* action has nothing in common with the employment of skirmishers in extended order for *demonstrative* purposes.

All the above-mentioned tactical errors of our Infantry are to be attributed to the fact of this distinction not having been sufficiently recognized in the press and hurry of the first moment, a distinction which has still been treated as of little consequence in the peace-training subsequent to the war, and which has now unexpectedly assumed decisive importance. This complete distinction however lies, in our opinion, in the radical difference between *demonstrative* and *decisive* action in battle with reference to the use of ground.

Whilst for instance in *demonstrative* combats a force is not only justified in suiting and subordinating its action to the ground, but also bound to do so, in a decisive battle it can only seek to avail itself of the ground as far as possible and to make the best use of it in the one decisive direction.

Our Infantry only acquired the former art at " field-exercise"; whilst in the "field-manœuvres" which generally represented only small affairs, we were usually of necessity forced to recognize the ground as the ruling element, on account of the weakness of the forces engaged, and in spite of the *"decisive ideas"* which were, in truth, rather kept in the background. Moreover the training preparatory to battle continued to be restricted to the drill-ground, or, at any rate, in the few days allotted to " division-exercises" there had not been sufficient opportunity or motive to get out of the old rut.

Thus at the decisive moment the really needful was wanting in spite of all individual perfection. Hence arose the practice on the part of our troops of splitting up for the purpose of seeking more favourable ground, hence the exaggerated extension of front, the confused interminglement; all intimately connected with an idea to which our field-exercise gave birth, that to take advantage of the ground is synonymous with plenty of space, freedom, and independence of higher direction.

So it came to this that the distinction made on principle between *field-exercise* and *drill* elevated to the utmost, so as to give the best possible returns in both domains, ended by producing difficulties in the battle-field which were only successfully overcome by the high intelligence of our leaders and the noble self-sacrifice of our men.

All honour to the energy and skill with which these battles were fought out, but we must not cite them as examples of correct tactics, and we may depend upon it that our probable adversaries of the future have already reflected upon this. A remedy is required, as we have already experienced, and which we have sought after in war; but now is specially the time to find it during the leisure of peace, and the whole army is anxiously searching for it.

Let us return to the question whether, by the tendency hitherto in force towards "all-sidedness" (making our men all equally good at everything), we shall attain our object. We think not—not at least until a length of time for training our men, which we can never indeed hope to command, is placed at our disposal.

A method of instruction which, with short service, aims at giving each recruit perfect, or at least sufficient, training in every branch, which is calculated to seek for results only in the sum of individual efforts instead of relying upon an organized division of labour, must and will very soon sink so far below the level of the requirements of war, which have in the present day so prodigiously risen, that it will produce no longer any satisfactory result whatever. It therefore behoves us to say, with concise decision, we require for the new tactics more practice in manœuvring than we have hitherto had ; and we must contrive to spare the time for it, as we can no longer expect the mass of individual soldiers to be equal to all the emergencies of war.

The value of individual instruction on its own account has increased, but it is no longer possible to arrive at this intrinsic accession of value by cramming the *individual soldier* with more material details; we must, on the contrary, rather do less in this way, so that, on the other hand, we may be able to get more out of the *body collectively*. The well-tested principles of training remain unaltered, only its material tasks and aims require to be changed. A satisfactory proficiency for *all* in the *necessary*, the greatest possible attainments for the *more gifted ones* in the *desirable*, branches of a soldier's trade; such must be the watch-word for a system of short service.

What things should come under the head of the *necessary* will hardly be a matter of doubt for anyone who has accompanied us through the first part of these studies.

The only possible *decisive* forms of combat, and of these two, of course most specially the *Offensive* will be of constant and unfailing occurrence, will come in the way of every soldier as long as war remains what it is; in contrast to these forms are the *indecisive*, proficiency in which is only *desirable*, although you will perhaps meet in them greater technical difficulties.

When now we go further into detail as to the knowledge and acquirements requisite for these forms of various degrees of importance, we must always distinguish between what is required of the individual and what of the body of which he is a member.

These questions, however, lead us to that of what should be the practice of our future "peace-school," whence it will appear that, as regards the daily routine of the service, it will not differ as much as, after all that has been said, one might suppose and fear, from our practice hitherto.   Let us first inquire what is *necessary ;* and in doing so we shall treat of the individual combatant.

The first thing we must demand of the soldier in every decisive combat is *discipline,* born of high personal energy.   Although this as a moral quality belongs to the domain of military *education*—a domain with which, as before remarked, we who treat only of the formal side of the question have nothing to do, still this fundamental condition of all great results must not here be passed over in silence, because we must allude to the outward means of developing it afforded by a rationally-conducted course of gymnastics, which, whilst giving a man complete control over his own limbs, accustoms him to the strictest regularity and steadiness in the ranks, to intelligent subordination.

A perfect familiarity with the use of arms is the second requirement for decisive combat.   The certain shot makes the good foot-soldier ; but the distances at which this sure aim comes into play in *decisive* action do not now-a-days, as a rule, exceed 400 paces.   In engagements where they are really in earnest, the real zone of activity for firearms lies in by far the greatest majority of cases between 450 and 150 paces.   The ranges, therefore, from 200 up to 400 paces constitute

the field in which the most thorough training in the use
of the rifle is necessary. It is of the greatest consequence that we should make our men as good shots
as possible at these distances, and at the same time
to take count of rapidity of fire, which plays so great
a part in decisive combats, as also of the various
nature of the marks to be aimed at (those under
cover or those moving on the skirmisher). But
the bullet is not yet the final argument. The soldier
should be accustomed from the very first to the use
of the bayonet, and this should be promoted by a
sensible and really serviceable system of bayonet
exercise, progressing by degrees to fencing, if for nothing
else, for its moral effect.

Skill in taking advantage of the ground is the third
quality which we should seek to develop for decisive
action by means of individual training. The power of
making use of or preparing for defence at pleasure every
accident of ground, whether for cover, however momentary, or to facilitate the action of our firearms, is, both for
decisively *offensive* situations as well as during the stage
of resistance of the *Defensive-Offensive*, an important
resource, and therefore one to be generally understood.
But in training our people to make use of it we should
be careful not to allow local considerations to interfere
arbitrarily with the assigned direction of personal action
in battle. To take advantage of accidents of ground
which happen to occur in the given direction of attack,
to know how to make the most of means of defence

which may chance to exist in the defensive position
assigned to occupy, this and this alone should be taught
and learnt.   Just in this consists the material difference
between our field training of the present day and that
of former times.   Extended order applied to the masses
can and should no longer allow that liberty of action
which, admitted as it was in our "field-exercise," was so
calculated to promote dispersion.

We now turn to the formal requirements of *decisive* action on a *body of troops.   The power of moving
surely and with cohesion in close order* stands first
and foremost as point of departure, and also as key-
stone of all action in battle.   *The ability to pass quickly
from one form of close order to another* (to perform
evolutions) and again to change from close to extended order and *vice versâ* (to extend, to close) come
next.

Individual action having become the rule of battle,
and tempting, as it does, to carelessness and disorder,
by way of counteraction, the greatest steadiness, the
most perfect order and precision amongst the masses
must be all the more insisted upon and enjoined.

But as the disciplining value of these exercises does
not consist in the quantity and complication of the
evolutions, but in the manner in which each is performed, the formations actually necessary in war will be
amply sufficient for our purpose, a subject to which we
must return further on.

Mobility, attention to orders, "fire-discipline" consti-

tute (*last not least* *) *the third* requirement to be considered in training troops for *decisive* action. The one
and only actual method of fighting, with its requirements, many of which still so new or at least unfamiliar
to us, even those of a purely formal character (different
movements, modes of firing, etc.) must be made a
second nature to our Infantry. Who will fail to comprehend that here is the field in which we can and must
spend a great part of the time which may be spared
from other work, and this can be done with advantage
even on the drill-ground, but especially on ground of
the most varied character.

*Lastly, a general acquaintance with the forms and
requirements of outpost duty*, imparted by practical instruction limited to what is absolutely necessary and
simplified to the utmost, will make our Infantry equal
to every emergency of the greater operations of war.†
All requirements which go beyond those just specially
mentioned as *necessary*, however *desirable* they may
otherwise be considered, cannot in our opinion be now-
a-days any longer met by the mass of the Infantry,
and they may be relinquished for them without prejudice to the general result, if on the other hand we
make up for it by giving all the more thorough training
to the chosen few.

We will now turn to what is required in this direc-

---

* *Sie*, in the original.—Tr.
† " Des grossen kriegrs," " la grande guerre," for which we have no equivalent expression. Of course every military reader understands the distinction made
by French and Germans between "great " and " little " war."—Tr.

tion. If, adhering with set purpose to the principle of classification, we select those young soldiers, and only those, who after their first year's service, *i. e.* when the autumn manœuvres have given them an idea of the daily life of war, have hitherto distinguished themselves from the mass, by greater power of comprehension, natural gifts, a lively interest in their profession, etc., and having thus selected them, push them on a step in advance of their comrades, such a course, as we before remarked, can only be advantageous. The range of study for the body of picked men to be formed thus to a certain extent in every company would comprise all that we have hitherto understood by the term "Field service" in its more limited sense. Above all, these men should be trained to taking advantage of the ground with greater *nicety*, if the expression is permissible, thus gaining an insight into the art of adapting their own action to the nature of the country, and learning at the same time to distinguish the comparatively rare cases in which this may be allowable. Patrol duties, as far as they can be performed by Infantry, the minor operations of war, also practice in executing works and tasks which under certain circumstances are required of Infantry, as for instance those of an engineering character,—all these things should be taught them both theoretically and practically; also, as far as it is feasible to do so, they should receive at least theoretical instruction as to their conduct in various situations of warfare, such as, for instance, investments, sieges, attack and defence of works,—subjects which, notwithstanding their importance, have hitherto been almost entirely neglected during peace.

It cannot be the aim or intention of these pages to enter into the details of carrying out our proposals. The "how" in these matters, in accordance with orders emanating from the highest source, is the special province of those from whom the "what" is required; and our task here only amounts to specifying in what that "what" consists. But we hope to have given all necessary proof in this dissertation that the demands which we are making upon our Infantry will ensure all *desirable* proficiency, even though on principle we relinquish any attempt to arrive at *universal* perfection (allseitige Ausbildung).

We already show the results of a soldier's musketry instruction in his discharge documents; we might surely also find place for such an expression as "qualified as leader of skirmishers," thus showing once for all the standard of instruction which we desire to attain.

Let us then resume our argument: considering how the demands upon our Infantry have increased, we must content ourselves under a system of short service with training our *masses* to the highest possible standard of efficiency in the tactical forms requisite for *decisive* action, and we must only aim at imparting *universal* proficiency to the more gifted members of a corps by giving them all the more careful instruction

even in the *indecisive* operations of war.   But even if
this principle be adopted everywhere practically as the
guiding one with reference to the course of training, we
shall still be compelled, in order to ensure real general
efficiency, to limit the quantity of *matter* taught to what
is *actually serviceable in war.*   It remains now, with
reference to the tactics of the present day, to cast a
glance upon this side of the question, so as to determine how narrow it may be allowable to make these
limits.

As far as concerns what we must necessarily require
of the individual soldier, it will be difficult to reduce
the *quantity of matter.*   At the same it must be confessed that by omitting the motion of "advance—
arms," a motion which can well be spared, much time
would be economised in individual instruction.*

The reduction to be effected in the formal training of
soldiers as a body will be of more consequence.

First it seems altogether allowable to abolish all
battalion evolutions hitherto executed at the commanding officer's word of command, as the battalion is no
longer a battle-unit, though it will still continue to be
one, for the march and for manœuvre.   It may be
considered sufficient for the warfare of the present
day, if the battalion concentrated in column can go
through its facings, interior movements, manual and
platoon, at the word of one officer.   But evolutions, *i. e.*

---

* Some of the motions of our own "Manual" might, I think, be omitted with
advantage.—Tr.

changes from one formation in close order to another, also the extension and re-assembling of the battalion, may without prejudice be executed at the word of command of the captains (now no longer required to lead divisions), commanding officers only giving the "cautions." *

If this were carried out, company drill in close-order movements would gain additional importance, and would require more time to be expended upon it, which will be all to the advantage of this important *battle-unit* (we purposely avoid the expression *tactical unit*).

All that we require of the battalions over and above this first groundwork belongs to the domain of "battle-exercise" of which we shall speak more at large when we treat of the instruction of officers.

We have further already pointed out in the first part of these studies that, with a view to simplifying our course to the utmost with regard to forms, we think that the retention of only one system of formation in rank and file is strongly to be recommended. It appears really quite unimportant at present whether in doing so our choice falls on the two or three deep formation.

Taking into consideration the fact that both methods have advantages and disadvantages which about balance one another, also the so much increased tendency to dispersion in the fighting of the present day, which

* This, amongst other changes, was recommended by me in a little book with a rather ambitious title, "A New System of Tactics for Infantry," published in 1867.—Tr.

reduces itself practically to only *single rank*, we should ourselves prefer the *more compact* three-deep formation —more compact by a third.

But this is only by the way. We enter into details of regulation no further than our "study" positively requires ; only, in opposition to some all too zealous innovators in this matter, we must define precisely our standpoint with regard to this subject, which it is not our province to discuss, by stating that we hardly want any part of the old drill regulations *altered,* first on account of the hundreds of thousands of reserve men, and again because we really do not think alteration required, but do wish to see *a good deal cut out.*

But we believe that a "peace-school," which aims at raising the standard of results whilst limiting the amount of things taught to what is necessary in war, will not fail to supply our leaders again, as in the past, with the solid and substantial materials suitable for "crowning the edifice" of future victories.

So much for the training of the soldier individually and collectively.

CHAPTER II.

THE more we are convinced, as expressed in the previous chapter, that modern tactical requirements force us to confine the formal training of the mass of our infantry to a minimum of *quantity*, so as to obtain to that extent at least the amount of desirable proficiency, all the more evident becomes the importance of the instruction of our officers. Their influence, which under the present conditions of increased difficulty has become all the more needful, can only make itself felt in a satisfactory manner if each one of them, according to his position, has the absolute faculty of judging every tactical situation, in which he may chance to find himself, with quick, just, and clear intelligence. To come to a right decision, always according to his position in the military hierarchy, as to the object of each engagement commenced, and thereupon to base his plans with judgment ; this it is which is required in the present day more than ever of every officer down to the lowest grade, and which can alone enable him to maintain his proper influence with his subordinates. The troops have only to fight when and where they receive

o

the order; but the officer in chief command, who from his post issues this order, bears the full and entire responsibility thereof. He must make up his mind as to what object he can and wishes to attain, for then, and then only, will he be in a position to make the best use of the means at his disposal.

Except the *fear* of responsibility, an officer of high or low degree can have no greater fault than to *forget* his responsibility.

Here we come to a dilemma which is in truth not easy to overcome. The sharpness, impetuosity, and energy which always are found united with quick, even hasty, determination, must be restrained; this sharp thirst for battle must give way to mature consideration, to the power of biding your time and of bearing delay; patience must be practised when the raging desire to get at the enemy has perhaps been raised to boiling heat by the aggravating hail of hostile bullets. And yet at the same time "the native hue of resolution" must not be "sicklied o'er with the pale cast of thought"—on the contrary the extreme of energy is required.

Is this not more than can be expected of man? Will not the attempt to obtain it lead to a lamentable *fiasco*—to want of decision and timidity, or at least to half-heartedness and lukewarmness?

And yet we believe that the venture must be made, as long as our officers are and continue to be what they now are. We must therefore bring them and the younger generation up to that spirit of self-sacrifice which shrinks from nothing, to that heroic daring which from the earliest days has added such wondrous leaves to the national laurels; but at the same time we wish to *train* them to somewhat calmer judgment. And further, whilst we may excuse men for going ahead themselves, and for allowing others to go ahead in war—and the more readily the lower their position—at the same time let us repress it when displayed at small cost at peace manœuvres. We have, by the way, no great fear that our "pluck will go to the devil" with such educational maxims.

One of our latest war-experiences also is that blind "élan" will not do much if we do not allow it to impose upon us. Calculated energy, the result of sound instruction, will amply replace qualities founded perhaps on the fool-hardiness generated by too hot blood.

Now, the main requirement for such a method of instruction by which a commanding officer (we choose purposely this comprehensive expression) may develop his own judgment, is an entire breach with that system of pre-arranged drill-ground combats, where even the second senior officer learns for the first time when receiving from his chief the order to attack, where he is to suppose the enemy to be; again the definite abolition of the distinction between manœuvring "across country" and on the "drill-ground," whenever we have to do with any phase of actual fighting.

As far as concerns practice in the mere formations of combat—for instance, the extension, movements, and firings of a line of skirmishers, the barrack-square and the drill-shed will be enough for the squad of recruits for whom alone this sort of thing can be wanted ; when we come to the company, however, we should no longer allow attacks to be made against "empty air." But the instruction of officers commences at once with "battle-practice," outside the barrack-gate and beyond the flat level of our present drill-grounds, always excepting the very beginners, who are hardly *boná fide* officers, and whom the captain has to instruct in the art of leading a division in close order, and such like.

This is the time to put in a word about the places which we from the force of habit are accustomed to search out for our military exercises, and the constantly increasing difficulty of discovering which in the neighbourhood of our garrisons appears to many calamitous, because the spectre of hut encampments *à la* Thiers appears in the background. But now really, considering the present tactical requirements of Infantry, so far from any advantage arising to us from having as open a plain as possible for this object, such ground would rather be unfavourable for training purposes. In the olden time, when the tactician sought out a plain for his *battle-field*, there was good sense and complete justification in selecting similar ground for *battle-practice* also ; but now-a-days, when the strategist

chooses his field of battle without in the least troubling
himself about the configuration of the ground, whilst
the tactician even gladly avoids a perfect flat, the
choice of places for practising battle-movements may
surely be less restricted. We have already in our first
chapter pointed out how mere drill—*i. e.*, the practice
of formations—has been or should be confined to much
smaller limits than heretofore, in consequence of the
later conditions of the altered nature of battle. Really,
the company alone now requires a drill-ground ; the
space necessary for the drill of a battalion—*i. e.*, for
its only remaining column-movements—may be very
much smaller than in former days.

It will be amply sufficient for its purpose if the length
of the space slightly exceeds the front of the battalion
in line, and if its breadth is a little more than three
times the front of the battalion in column. These
measurements are, however, far below those to which
we now pretend, and they are such as the yard of every
one of our newer barracks would afford for a battalion
on its peace-footing.

Everything connected with battalion-exercises which
goes beyond this point can no longer be counted as
drill, but is rather included under the head of "battle-
practice," for which we no longer require perfectly level
ground. But as soon as we give up this requirement,
we shall still find undulating ground (only let it be dry)
in the immediate neighbourhood of our large garrisons
—*i. e.*, towns, which will serve as fields for the "battle-

practice " of our infantry—such ground being, moreover,
as a rule not such as is sought after by co-operative
agricultural associations.

With such undulating country (and no matter if here
and there in cultivation or intersected by smaller and
greater obstacles) for our " exercise-grounds," that distinction of which we complained in our first chapter
between *field-service* and *field-exercise* will melt away
with the greatest ease in face of an increased unity of
idea ; and the more varied the ground the more will it
tend to develop the tactical judgment and the understanding both of the young officer and of the older
commander.

But if we wish our " battle-exercises " to meet this
end, they must be made subordinate to a clear and
definite idea from the very first moment of entering
upon this field of instruction, a condition with which
we cannot dispense even on the most platform-like
drill-ground, if the battalion be broken up or thrown
into skirmishing order as for " battle."

By this we do not mean that the commander should
plague himself with extensive *general* and *special* ideas,
but we do mean that when a body of troops is to
engage an imaginary enemy, his supposed position
should be pointed out to it, if an attack is intended ;
the supposed direction of his movements should be
indicated, if it is proposed to remain on the defensive ;
the point which he is assumed to have reached should
be shown, if a counter-attack is planned ; and, finally,

his whereabouts should be made known, if a mere demonstration is purposed; and all this should be done clearly and definitely.

If the ground does not furnish us with clearly suitable points of vantage, we may content ourselves with marking the spots in the simplest possible manner by using adjutants and non-commissioned officers to make the limits of the enemy's position, the point of attack, or the line of the enemy's advance clear to the eye.

If only the "exercise-ground" is not absolutely flat, the battle-pictures may in this manner be much varied in kaleidoscope fashion, and the greatest possible variety in detail is desirable together with complete simplicity in the main features, particularly if the younger officers are to learn anything. It is only by seeing this from every possible point of view and by doing it in every possible manner that our sight is so sharpened as to recognize quickly the right course of action, and this is just what we have to aim at for actual warfare.

There are very few men who judge things more clearly when under fire, and those are exceptional persons whose understanding, which, before seemed to slumber, gathers strength amidst the enemy's bullets. *Habit* is the best security for keeping the mind clear even in press of danger.

Just as with the private soldier the habit of discipline makes obedience into a second nature, even in the most trying moments, so with the officer the habit of observing ground must make a correct judgment as to making the most of it, become to him a second nature.

This end, however, can only be obtained if a great number of as varied fights as possible are worked out on the practice-ground and *discussed concisely and instructively.*

As certainly as in actual warfare a pause of rest for re-establishing order must follow every attack successfully made or repulsed, so on the practice-ground, after one attack has been made, one position quickly occupied, the troops under inspection may surely without prejudice be led on to perform a second, a third, and even more operations of quite a different character, without its being necessary for these various practices, though executed in one day, to have any connection with one another. It must only be made clear to both officers and men that " now something else is coming."

In this manner, for instance, a battalion will easily be able to represent in a course of eight or ten exercises some thirty battle-pictures with ever-varying shades, and this even on ground affording comparatively little change. Every time the direction of attack is somewhat altered, the mode of advance of the line of skirmishers, the manner of occupying the ground and so forth are modified, and the most varied changes in detail are developed on a foundation of sound principles.

By these means both field officers and captains will be educated to the correct way of taking advantage of

ground in each specified direction, thus gaining that
quickness of eye which will afterwards prevent all
wavering in the actual emergency, and which will
result in making them do the right thing instinctively.

Moreover, just as in this manner we may train our
people to the exigencies of *decisive* battle, so may we
train them after the same fashion to the *temporising*
combat.

The same place of exercise may be used, without
extending our "ideas" much further, for practising
the battalion in advanced and rear-guard actions or in
reconnoissance; lastly, it may serve to represent the
"intermediate stage between two decisive situations,"
again helping to form a correct judgment.

We will now say of the "what" just what we before
said of the "how." * By such a course of training in
the battalion, the regiment, even in the brigade; and
we maintain only and solely by such a course shall we
arrive at forming the judgment of every officer according to his station, so as to enable him to come to the
important decision which will be constantly required of
him in war, as to whether he should keep his troops
back or commit them to action, and at once to choose
the right course.

By such numerous and varied "battle-exercises," we
shall teach the young officer to be kept in hand and
the elder officer to keep in hand. Each will learn to
form a right estimate of the value of the detachment

* See p. 189.—Tr.

under his command with reference to the whole force,
and to subordinate himself to the higher object in view.
By this means also we shall recover that tactical precision once the pride and strength of our army, but
which has, we cannot deny, abandoned us in these
latter years and during the late campaigns.

That long-proved "fire-discipline," dating from the
time of the great Frederick, which has worked such
wonders for us, is still just as necessary for us as it was
then and at all times ; only it no longer depends on
our men but on our lieutenants. The independence of
the individual soldier in action has since those old
times wonderfully augmented, hence the difficulty of
controlling him has extraordinarily increased; but the
necessity of control remains the same now as ever.
And as in this way with the task of the lieutenant with
reference to his division, so on account of the altered
character of command in action the task of the captain
with reference to his subalterns, of the battalion-commander with reference to his captains (who have gained
greater independence), and so upwards, has each individual's task become very much more onerous, whilst
the value, importance, and necessity of each have not
thereby been in the least diminished.

Even so far back as that, the great king was obliged
to oppose with energetic reprimands a habit of dispersion "which leads to this, that the common soldier
decides the battle ; and this is an every-day affair
(journalier)." Now we shall not be misunderstood if

we say : it is also "journalier" for the lieutenant or captain to decide the battle ; such being the favourite theme of our innovators of the present day, whose passionate ardour would lead them to give no chance in this way to the battalion commander, not to mention higher authorities.

We learn from the experience of war that if *peace-habits* have not prepared us to meet this difficulty, *incorporating, as it were, in our flesh and blood the conviction of the necessity of maintaining the influence of the higher and highest authority*, the force of momentary circumstances will be stronger than all theory and all good will.

There is truly something great in that universal strife to go *forward* which has animated even the smallest detachment, and it is hardly necessary to clear ourselves of the suspicion that we wish to suppress this feeling, but if this noble sentiment is to conduce to the general result instead of uselessly evaporating, as it often does, in isolated deeds of heroism, the conviction must be carefully fostered beforehand in peace, that intelligent obedience stands even before dash, and that in battle the commander-in-chief will give an opportunity at the right moment for every man to satisfy his thirst for action.

Thus officers in high command will no longer have to fear that if they hold back even in critical moments, their conduct will be misjudged by their subordinates, and those in a lower position will learn that by having a little patience they will reap all the larger crop of laurels.

. So we repeat that the system of training for our officers centres itself in "battle-exercises" of a practical nature, answering to the requirements of modern tactics, and no longer recognising any difference between "field-exercise" and "field-practice." We know well that this is not all that can be said upon the matter, and that there are claims upon officers both of high and low degree which they must meet in order to be fully competent for their respective duties. But the first thing to be thought of for them, as for the rank and file, is to prepare them for the universal, the inevitable, the constantly recurring exigencies of warfare; afterwards attempting to give them as officers thorough efficiency in all the other phases of military action.

So these "battle-exercises" are the kernel round which group themselves on one side the *greater manœuvres* to which we shall devote a special chapter, on the other side the *smaller manœuvres* for training in the minor tasks of war (des grossen Krieges).

These latter furnish a special field for work to our younger officers, who, whilst making their first appearance as instructors upon it, have the opportunity of themselves learning so much.

In these little operations the judgment develops itself, the spirit of self-reliance is engendered, which spirit they have again to school themselves to sacrificing elsewhere of their own free will and from conviction to the claims of a larger unit.

Here the opportunity for acting on his own responsibility offers itself to the young officer, here the fruits of his own work manifest themselves, to gather which fruit is the natural desire of every mortal. The small proportions of the work which he is here called upon to direct will make him comprehend all the more fully and unmistakably the necessity for subordination and unity of command in work of larger proportions.

Here, too, he will learn on a small scale, whilst distinguishing between more and less favourable ground, and whilst teaching his select men to do so, how every sort of ground may on a larger scale be utilized, and at the same time he will acquire the capacity of coming on every occasion to the right determination.

If, as we go on, we accustom the learner to hostile action by practising one party against another, these *little manœuvres*, more or less useful even for superior officers, according to the strength of the forces engaged, form quite fairly part of a system of education for officers. As far as garrison arrangements will permit, we must also endeavour to carry on these exercises, particularly such as have reference to *field* and *outpost* duties, with mixed detachments of cavalry and infantry, before the corps proceeds to take part in the *great manœuvres* which will give the finishing touch to its training.

We do not propose to ourselves here, any more than

when treating of the *soldier individually and collectively*, to enter into details. Here, as there, we are only called upon to specify clearly and broadly the point of view from which the object aimed at should be regarded, and the ways and means for attaining it ; the work itself is the province of the workman.

We only wish to add one thing more. The "education of the officer" cannot be considered complete so long as it is confined to the narrow limits of a number of "exercises," however practically conducted. Theoretical study must, of course, keep pace with them. We are all the more anxious not to omit mention of this *personal work* of every officer as a pedestal to the edifice of our performances of quite equal value to the other, because otherwise a misunderstanding might easily arise, and we might be supposed not to assign their full value to *theoretical studies*, thus undermining the theoretical study which we have devoted to the very *study* now before us. The "method of application," to which we owe such great progress, will furnish rich and ample materials for this study, even to our youngest comrades. May they continue to use them as fairly as ever ; then for them will the good fruit of practice ripen upon the tree of sound theory.

CHAPTER III.

It remains now to cast a last glance on that part of our system of peace-instruction where officers and men, having undergone the preparatory course advocated, are brought up in company to the highest stage of their efficiency, and as the season draws to a close, are to prove in the field of the *great manœuvres* to the chiefs in high and in highest command, lastly to the Imperial Commander himself, that the army is equal to its task.

There are three objects which we strive to attain by these *great manœuvres:* Mutual acquaintance between the different corps and arms, and the power of giving mutual support, are to be promoted and encouraged ; officers of all ranks have to learn how to make use of what they have already practised in face of an adversary who on his side is not idle. Both the soldier and the corps must get acquainted with and accustomed to the daily routine of life in the field.

In order to meet this triple demand, our "divisional autumnal manœuvres " have already been divided into "field" and "outpost" *practice,* "field manœuvres

with two forces opposed to one another," and
"manœuvres of the entire division." We must examine this tripartition somewhat more closely from the
standpoint of war as at present carried on.

It must be recognized as a rule hitherto usually
followed that the troops assembled for these annual
exercises do not exceed the strength of a division.
Royal reviews, at which the two divisions of an army-
corps, or great autumnal manœuvres, at which at the
outside two army-corps were concentrated, are, as we
know, of rare occurrence, occurring exceptionally,
often after an interval of some years, of which the
Guard corps has alone not to complain, in consequence
of the convenient arrangement of its quarters. The
division of all arms forming now the *battle-unit*, at any
rate by assembling it annually, as is done on principle,
the basis at least of a system of instruction calculated
to meet even the highest demands is provided.

Nevertheless, we cannot fail to remark that here
also our old habits are affected by the requirements of
modern tactics, which seem to make a modification in
the division of time allowed to the different exercises
urgently necessary. According to present regulations
the division, as such, has only three (even sometimes
two) days for the so-called "divisional-exercises"
(manœuvres of the entire division). Of these one is
taken up with the divisional *parade*, so that the division
is only assembled under command of its general for
united battle-practice twice, or may be once a year.

Considering, however, the great tasks which devolve upon an infantry division in modern battle this scanty allowance of time would appear much too small.

Twelve battalions and twenty-four guns, without reckoning the cavalry regiment, represent, even in the battles of masses which take place in the present epoch, such an imposing force that the fact of its being employed, successfully or otherwise, may well exert a decisive effect upon the course of the whole action. The attack even of a single division properly led by the commander, and well executed by the troops, may incline the scales in our favour amidst the conflict of hundreds of thousands which has raged doubtfully for hours; the overthrow of one single division in a defensive position may tear a gap in our line which can never again be closed. That the *division*, being the smallest independent unit on which a commander can reckon for the decisive stroke which he meditates, should be in thoroughly efficient working order, is a necessary condition, not only for the great tactical, but also for the strategical result. The "division" represents to the commander-in-chief a constant mathematical expression of offensive and defensive force upon which he may base his higher and final calculations with incontestable security.

This was the case formerly, and so it must continue to be; but it has become more difficult to carry out; yes, very much more difficult, on account of the loosening effect of the battle of the present day.

Much steady practice is required, unless we wish to see what may easily happen in the heat of such battles as we have now, whole divisions melt away, like snow under a March sun, *useless because not under control of the one commander.*

We have already often pointed out in general terms the dangers of dispersion to which the tactics of the present age may so easily lead; the division welded together into unity by *habits acquired during peace* is the rock upon which that dreaded wave must break.

If in the old times of column-tactics, the battalion mass was the symbol of united force and concentrated energy, constantly reforming, as it did, its dense array, so in these times, when the nature of battle occasions a greater dispersion the smaller the body, this necessary *conviction of strength* is only inherent in the larger bodies; in none more thoroughly than in the *division*. It is the smallest "fighting-assemblage" which under modern conditions of war can of itself produce a decisive result.

The battalion, the regiment, the brigade, these are all important intermediate bodies, each of which will, as far as it can, endeavour to keep itself together, but each of which will possibly find itself compelled to fight *without depth*; the division with its framework of artillery is the first to present the cohesion of an organic body. It appeared to us necessary to enter rather at length into this pre-eminent consequence of the infantry-division in modern battle, so as to deduce from thence all the more decisively the importance of its training during peace.

Once allow the full extent of its value, and you cannot deny that to attain to it more than two days' work per annum are required.

Here, again, perhaps what we before said about the relation which the soldier bears to the corps to which he belongs applies, only one step higher ; the efficiency of the division is not entirely based upon the sum of efficiency of all its separate battalions. Twelve battalions, four regiments, two brigades, may all have been thoroughly trained beforehand in " battle-practice;" yet when united into a division they may do little good as such, they may even get it and thereby also themselves into a scrape, if they are not accustomed to subordinate themselves completely to the undivided command of their divisional general. The reason is this, that with the present conditions of strength even a brigade can only exceptionally find itself in a position to represent *by itself* more than one situation in a combat (an attack, a defence, &c.), and that a division is the smallest body which has the power of going through the whole fight, including "introduction" and "victory." But the division itself, being only the first and smallest battle unit, must therefore also learn to take its share in action in a manner suited to the circumstances as the part of a whole ; and for this reason it also requires the kind of "battle-practice" in which, being employed as a unit for a limited purpose actually

assigned or supposed by the commander-in-chief, it has
to a certain extent to represent only one definite situation of battle. With demands of, as it appears to us,
such unquestionably two-fold character as regards
our training, we must declare that we consider it extremely desirable that the annual period of three days
now allowed for the exercises of the united division
should be extended to *at least six*, and, if larger assem-
blages of troops take place, wherever possible to *nine
real working days*. Of these it is certainly desirable
that *one* should be set apart expressly for a *parade* of
the whole division, if such cannot conveniently be
tacked on to a "battle-practice." Such military dis-
plays on a large scale impart both to the corps and to
the individual, to a greater extent than is generally
supposed, the feeling of "all belonging together-ness,"
the consciousness of strength, the certainty that "there
are a great lot of us." They also tell well upon the
great public, which rarely but on such occasions has
an opportunity of raising its spirits by a contemplation
of the nation's power. At these parades, and often
only by means of these parades, do the different arms
make each other's acquaintance, outwardly at least,
and come to know of one another, what is the size of a
cavalry regiment, of an infantry battalion, and so
forth ; the private soldier often never seeing these
bodies together except on such occasions. The other
five or eight days we should like to see equally divided
between the kind of "battle-exercise" in which the

division comes into play as an united whole to carry out a definite portion of a supposed action, and that in which it goes through the fight independently and isolated.

For the first object the ground itself will usually supply the necessary points to mark the position or movements of the supposed enemy, or such points may easily be indicated, as we before remarked when treating of "battle-exercises;" for the latter purpose the regulations upon an "indicated enemy" in the "imperial orders" come into force. Here, likewise, again we have only to speak of "what" is desirable, leaving confidently the "how" to the decision of those in command. We only wish to draw attention to the importance of combining with the above-mentioned exercises, as can easily be done, the most varied practice possible in bringing the division into line of battle from one or from more columns of route at the same time.

It will be objected to the wish here expressed for multiplying the exercises of the united division, that this can only be accomplished at the cost of the two other above-mentioned exercises, both also doubtless very important branches of instruction, without an increased expenditure of time and particularly of money.

Perhaps, however, we may succeed in meeting this objection by the following arguments. The three days' "field" and "out-post" exercises have for their object, as denoted by their designation, actually merely the incidents of out-post duty,[*] and of the minor operations of war which, with a few isolated exceptions, are developed from it alone, as we have all experienced in the last great wars. At our "peace-exercises," however, it has hitherto been the custom, in order to furnish a motive for the intended out-post position, to conceive "ideas" in the three days, often of the most wonderful description, derived from times long past (for instance, forced[†] foraging expeditions, convoy-escorts, and such like), which culminated at length in scuffles between small detachments, which it is only to be hoped that our army will now-a-days avoid.

On this account it appears to us that we may, without prejudice, give up these days as an independent cycle of exercises, and that it will be a more practical course to unite the out-post exercises as far as they cannot be practised beforehand in "mixed" garrisons, with the great manœuvres of the division. If, for instance, at the end of each "battle-exercise" of the entire division, which of itself would not take up more than, at the outside, two or three hours' time, a small portion of the division were told off as rear-guard of the enemy supposed to be repulsed, or as his advanced

---

[*] "Sicherheitsdienst," literally "safety-service," *i. e.* the duty of ensuring an army against surprise. There is no expression in our language actually equivalent. That used in the text is the nearest approach.—Ta.

[†] The expression is, I am aware, not good English, but perhaps it may be pardoned for want of a letter and as preferable to a long paraphrase. Besides, a "forced reconnoissance" is an accepted military term. Why not then speak of "forced foraging"?—Ta.

guard, supposing him victorious, and were ordered to take up a line of out-posts consistent with the "idea," whilst another fraction of the division were directed to ensure its security in accordance with the supposed situation, doubtless nothing but advantage could accrue from such a course.

The out-post duty itself will appear more like reality, because founded on conditions more nearly akin to war ; there will be the more ample time for all its incidents after the short day's work, because its main difficulties arise at night ; as for the division itself, the bivouac, which has become indispensable, will, if only the general-staff officer shows a little dexterity, on this occasion, take the place of a long march, instead of a short march to cantonments or in the morning from cantonments which it would have formerly had.   When the division assembles the next morning, the "idea" which has previously directed the conduct of the troops which may happen to occupy the out-post position of course ceases to be in force, having from the first not affected those which took no part in the practice. Whilst thus the "out-post exercises" are suppressed, as an independent feature in the autumn manœuvres, the time remains intact for the detachment-exercises which accustom officers, at first on a small scale, to the counter-action of the enemy ; but we should not hesitate to shorten this period in favour of the exercises of the entire division, if the pretext for doing so is afforded by determining upon subsequent greater manœuvres for which the *division* must thus be all the more carefully prepared.

We shall come now by a roundabout way which takes us momentarily beyond the limits of Infantry-tactics to the necessity for having these greater manœuvres or concentrations as frequently as possible. We have hitherto spoken of the exercises of an Infantry-division, without taking into consideration the fact that, according to our custom hitherto, a number of batteries and a force of cavalry have been attached during the period of exercise to the two divisions of an army corps on the peace footing far in excess of the proportion for war. It has been hitherto allowable for us to take no notice of this circumstance, because it had no material effect upon the method and design of exercise of the division on a peace footing which still remained in substance an *Infantry-division.* The number of guns did not differ greatly from that *actually* at the disposal of a division in war,* and the general result is not much affected by whether the available surplus is looked upon as performing the part of division or of corps-artillery. The superfluous cavalry brigade also was, at all events, not calculated to affect the suitable training of the divisional infantry, whether it were appropriated by the divisional commander to serve his own purposes, or whether he considered it as by chance in his neighbourhood during the action.

---

* A Prussian field battery only turns out four guns and thirty-seven horses in peace time. —Tr.

But viewing this matter from a cavalry stand-point it bears a different aspect. The following experience of the late most instructive war, more perhaps than any other, strikes the tactical inquirer : the rush (if we may so say) made of late by this arm to resume once more its position on equal terms with the sister arms even in actual battle—a field in theory closed against it, and from which it was considered to be quite shut out. The part which it played on the German side with so much distinction—that of *veil*—appears to it now in peace no longer sufficient, and it again aims at doing in addition to this its old work as *wedge*. It appears to promise itself, thereby digging its own grave, the recovery of that influence of which it has been robbed by the rapidity and accuracy of rifle fire, through the looseness of infantry formation which that very fire has promoted. To be able to break in among the enemy's "footmen," scattered as they will be in thin lines, with masses of rapidly-moving horsemen following one another, squadron upon squadron, this is the dream which our cavalry have brought back by way of *war-experience* to the peace-garrisons, and to realize which they now ask for mass-training during peace.

It is not our part to inquire in this "study" into the pros and cons for these aspirations, which only interest us here, as perhaps it is more likely that in consequence thereof a modification of the autumn arrangements may result. But if the annual concentration of a cavalry division within the army-corps for independent exercise is to be the invariable rule, the annual concentration of the army-corps itself, even if only for a few days' general exercise, must in consequence soon appear absolutely necessary, so as to give this body, which will then alone have the power of practising the employment of the three arms in battle, the opportunity for instruction indispensably necessary.

But also quite independent of this influence upon our peace-training, which is perhaps more a matter of chance, and the necessity for which will not be absolutely admitted everywhere, it will be impossible much longer to avoid recognising that, with the actual conditions of warfare, a more frequent assemblage of the larger masses of troops is indispensable to the thorough and complete preparation for every emergency of our own and of every other army, and that this measure cannot be delayed any longer without mischief.

Do what you will, these exercises will be very far indeed behind what is wanted to represent the realities of war, but the performances of peace and the requirements of war must at least approximate, if any profit is to be obtained, and if there is not to be a pure waste of strength.

Again and again we consider it necessary to give our warning against the tendency to view the performances of large bodies as simply the sum of the performances of their smaller composite parts; on the contrary, we should be inclined to maintain that the former are with regard to difficulty as the square of the latter.

Considering the migration of peoples which our modern wars represent, we cannot consider it an exorbitant demand that at least as many battalion, squadron and battery-*cadres*, without attempting even to raise them to a war strength, may temporarily be assembled for our peace manœuvres as must be assumed to be engaged against one another in the smallest battles of the present day. If also financial considerations should not admit of such comparatively considerable concentrations to take place yearly, as in the time of Frederick the Great, when, in the four " inspections" (districts) a fourth always of the whole peace-army was assembled, an army much stronger than the present one in proportion to the size of state at that time ; it is yet excessively desirable that the rule should be that every other year there should either be a concentration of the whole of the troops of an " inspection" or of the army-corps.

These great manœuvres need indeed never last very long, their object being, in substance, only to give the troops an idea of how they are handled in masses, and to form officers for high command, who, if only these reviews became of regular occurrence, would, in the course of their service, have repeated opportunities for accustoming themselves to what is required of them in this respect.

Even the Potsdam reviews, which all Europe used

to attend, lasted only three days each time, and although always taking place on almost precisely the same ground with the same number of thirty-eight battalions and fifty squadrons, they show so much variety, a thing more difficult to attain then even than now, that not one of the twenty-four battle-exercises in the fourteen successive annual courses which have come down to us is like another. If so it must be then, this example may at least set our minds at rest so far as to convince us that such exercises need not be made monotonous, even if we were compelled to conduct them for a long series of years from a standing camp on one and the same ground.

But the following " idea " comes out pretty often in the reports of these field-days just alluded to—one to be recommended as useful by way of change, " the next day his Majesty showed how such an attack (or something of the sort) might have been been better managed."

Considerations of expense may (and of this we have no means of judging) induce our rulers to confine such manœuvres to certain localities, and may render the formation of camps necessary. But even if such should be the case, this measure would not be subject to those objections which one often hears urged against it, always supposing the camps to be used only for a short time, and by one and the same body of troops. But we hope, in the interests of a healthy, soldier-like life, that our army may be spared the trial of having its greater manœuvres, especially those of the division, tied down on principle to such camps. We should be sorry to exchange our old privilege of the shifting canton- ment, of free intercourse with nature, as we might almost say, for an arrangement which, if continued permanently, would infallibly be fatal to the healthy circulation, and would poison the fresh and cheery spirit of our army.

Once more; if it must be so, and if by no other means the great concentrations of troops, which are so urgently necessary, can be managed, at least, let the measure only be applied to these, and in every case only for a short time.

We return to our starting point in these studies.

To take early account of the requirements of the new tactics in our "peace-school" must, we thought, be recognized as a *necessity* not to be deferred ; changes merely of a formal nature could not be considered suf- ficient for this purpose. They would burden the short period for peace-training with an additional *quantity* of work which could not be done justice to in face of the extraordinary rise of the standard of *quality*. We were compelled, on the contrary, to admit that the absolute amount of training in externals must be reduced to a minimum, both for the individual and the corps, so that, what is of much more importance now-a-days, the thorough proficiency of each man in what he is actually taught, might be attained.

The principle of classification, with regard to the

higher training of the mass of our Infantry, thus showed itself to be the necessary consequence, and one which would answer all demands—a principle which would not make the efficiency of a corps depend solely upon the efficiency of each of its members. But, in order to be equal even to the highest exigencies, it was, we thought, incumbent upon us to accustom the officers of all ranks to their war duties, by giving them the most varied "battle-exercises" in the field, and thereby training them to rapid and just tactical judgment respecting the "what" as well as the "how."

Finally, remembering, as we did, that the true fruit of even the most brilliant bloom of peace-instruction will only be seen to ripen on the battle-field, we thought it advisable to recommend manœuvres in great masses, with, at least, a resemblance to war, from which alone we dare to hope that we may in *peace* get the best possible idea of *Battle*.

THE END.

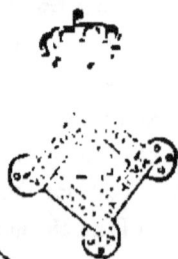

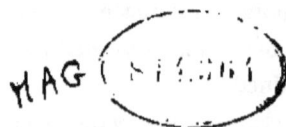

BRADBURY, AGNEW, & CO., PRINTERS, WHITEFRIARS, LONDON.

A CATALOGUE OF

HENRY S. KING & CO.'S PUBLICATIONS.

i

SOME BIOGRAPHICAL SKETCHES OF THE XVIIth CENTURY. By W. D. Christie, C.B., Author of 'The Life of the First Earl of Shaftesbury.'

ii

THE PORT OF REFUGE; or, Counsel and Aid to Shipmasters in Difficulty, Doubt, or Distress. By Manley Hopkins, Author of 'A Handbook of Average,' 'A Manual of Insurance,' &c. Subjects:— The Shipmaster's Position and Duties. Agents and Agency. Average. Bottomry, and other Means of Raising Money. The Charter-Party, and Bill-of-Lading. Stoppage in transitu; and the Shipowner's Lien. Collision.

iii

THE PEARL OF THE ANTILLES; or, an Artist in Cuba. By Walter Goodman. Crown 8vo.

iv

WHY AM I A CHRISTIAN? Crown 8vo.

v

THE ROMANTIC ANNALS OF A NAVAL FAMILY. By Mrs. Arthur Traherne. Crown 8vo. 10s. 6d.

vi

THE SUNNY AND CLOUDY DAYS OF MDME. LA VICOMTESSE DE LEOVILLE-MEILHAN. By Mdme. La Vicomtesse de Kermadec. Crown 8vo.

vii

SHORT LECTURES ON THE LAND LAWS. Delivered before the Working Men's Institute. By T. Leah Wilkinson. Crown 8vo. cloth limp, 2s.

viii

STUDIES AND ROMANCES. By H. Schütz-Wilson. One vol. crown 8vo. 7s. 6d.

ix

THE RELIGIOUS HISTORY OF IRELAND: Primitive, Papal, and Protestant; including the Evangelical Missions, Catholic Agitations, and Church Progress, of the last Half-Century. By James Godkin, Author of 'Ireland and her Churches' &c. 1 vol. 8vo.

X

MEMOIR AND LETTERS OF SARA COLERIDGE. Two vols. crown 8vo. With Portraits.

XI

LOMBARD STREET. A Description of the Money Market. By WALTER BAGEHOT. Large crown 8vo. 7s. 6d.

XII

POLITICAL WOMEN. By SUTHERLAND MENZIES. Two vols. post 8vo.

XIII

EGYPT AS IT IS. By Herr HEINRICH STEPHAN, the German Postmaster-General. Crown 8vo. With a new Map of the Country.

XIV

IMPERIAL GERMANY. By FREDERIC MARTIN, Author of 'The Statesman's Year-Book' &c.

XV

THE GOVERNMENT OF THE NATIONAL DEFENCE. By JULES FAVRE. One vol. demy 8vo.

XVI

'ILÁM ÉN NÁS. Historical Tales and Anecdotes of the Times of the Early Khalifahs. Translated from the Arabic Originals, by Mrs. GODFREY CLERK, Author of 'The Antipodes and Round the World.' Crown 8vo.

XVII

IN STRANGE COMPANY; or, The Note Book of a Roving Correspondent. By JAMES GREENWOOD, 'The Amateur Casual.' Crown 8vo.

XVIII

THEOLOGY AND MORALITY. Being Essays by the Rev. J. LLEWELLYN DAVIES. One vol. 8vo. 7s. 6d.

XIX

THE RECONCILIATION OF RELIGION AND SCIENCE. Being Essays by the Rev. J. W. FOWLE, M.A. One vol. 8vo. 10s. 6d.

XX

A NEW VOLUME OF ACADEMIA ESSAYS. Edited by the Most Reverend ARCHBISHOP MANNING.

XXI

THE FAYOUM; OR, ARTISTS IN EGYPT. A Tour with M. Gérôme and others. By J. LENOIR. Translated by Mrs. CASHEL HOEY. Crown 8vo. cloth. Illustrated. 7s. 6d.

XXII

TENT LIFE WITH ENGLISH GYPSIES IN NORWAY. By HUBERT SMITH. In 8vo. cloth. Five full-page Engravings and thirty-one smaller Illustrations: with Map of the Country, showing Routes. Price 21s.

XXIII

THE GATEWAY TO THE POLYNIA; or, a Voyage to Spitsbergen. By Captain JOHN C. WELLS, R.N. In 8vo. cloth. Profusely illustrated.

XXIV

A WINTER IN MOROCCO. By AMELIA PERRIER. Large crown 8vo. Illustrated, price 10s. 6d.

XXV

An AUTUMN TOUR in the UNITED STATES and CANADA. By Lieut.-Colonel JULIUS GEORGE MEDLEY. Crown 8vo. price 8s.

XXVI

IRELAND IN 1872. A Tour of Observation, with Remarks on Irish Public Questions. By Dr. JAMES MACAULAY. Crown 8vo. 7s. 6d.

XXVII

THE GREAT DUTCH ADMIRALS. By JACOB DE LIEFDE. Crown 8vo. Illustrated, price 6s.

XXVIII

NEWMARKET AND ARABIA. An Examination of the Descent of Racers and Coursers. By ROGER D. UPTON. Crown 8vo. Illustrated, price 9s.

XXIX

FIELD AND FOREST RAMBLES OF A NATURALIST IN NEW BRUNSWICK. With Notes and Observations on the Natural History of Eastern Canada. By A. LEITH ADAMS, M.A. &c., Author of 'Wanderings of a Naturalist in India' &c. &c. In 8vo. cloth. Illustrated. 14s.

XXX

BOKHARA: ITS HISTORY AND CONQUEST. By Professor ARMINIUS VÁMBÉRY, of the University of Pesth, Author of 'Travels in Central Asia' &c. Demy 8vo. price 18s.

'We conclude with a cordial recommendation of this valuable book. In former years Mr. Vámbéry gave ample proofs of his powers as an observant, easy, and vivid writer. In the present work his moderation, scholarship, insight, and occasionally very impressive style, have raised him to the dignity of an historian.'— *Saturday Review.*

Almost every page abounds with composition of peculiar merit, as well as with an account of some thrilling event more exciting than any to be found in an ordinary work of fiction.'—*Morning Post.*

A work compiled from many rare, private, and unavailable manuscripts and records, which consequently cannot fail to prove a mine of delightful Eastern lore to the Oriental scholar.'—*Liverpool Albion.*

xxxi

OVER VOLCANOES; OR, THROUGH FRANCE AND SPAIN IN 1871. By A. Kingsman. Crown 8vo. 10s. 6d.

'The writer's tone is so pleasant, his language is so good, and his spirits are so fresh, buoyant, and exhilarating, that you find yourself inveigled into reading, for the thousand-and-first time, a description of a Spanish bull-fight.'—*Illustrated London News.*

'The adventures of our tourists are related with a good deal of pleasantry and humorous dash, which make the narrative agreeable reading.'—*Public Opinion.*

'A work which we cordially recommend to such readers as desire to know something of Spain as she is to-day. Indeed, so fresh and original is it, that we could have wished that it had been a bigger book than it is.'—*Literary World.*

xxxii

ALEXIS DE TOCQUEVILLE. Correspondence and Conversations with Nassau W. Senior from 1833 to 1859. Edited by Mrs. M. C. M. Simpson. 2 vols. large post 8vo. 21s.

'Another of those interesting journals in which Mr. Senior has, as it were, crystallised the sayings of some of those many remarkable men with whom he came in contact.'—*Morning Post.*

'A book replete with knowledge and thought.'—*Quarterly Review.*

'An extremely interesting book, and a singularly good illustration of the value which, even in an age of newspapers and magazines, memoirs have and will always continue to have for the purposes of history.'—*Saturday Review*

xxxiii

JOURNALS KEPT IN FRANCE AND ITALY, FROM 1848 TO 1852. With a Sketch of the Revolution of 1848. By the late Nassau William Senior. Edited by his Daughter, M. C. M. Simpson. In 2 vols. post 8vo. 24s.

'The present volume gives us conversations with some of the most prominent men in the political history of France and Italy . . . as well as with others whose names are not so familiar or are hidden under initials. Mr. Senior has the art of inspiring all men with frankness, and of persuading them to put themselves unreservedly in his hands without fear of private circulation.'—*Athenæum.*

'The book has a genuine historical value.'—*Saturday Review.*

'No better, more honest, and more readable view of the state of political society during the existence of the second Republic could well be looked for.'—*Examiner.*

XXXIV

A MEMOIR OF NATHANIEL HAWTHORNE, with Stories now first Published in this Country. By H. A. Page. Large post 8vo. 7s. 6d.

'The Memoir is followed by a criticism of Hawthorne as a writer ; and the criticism, though we should be inclined to dissent from particular sentiments, is, on the whole, very well written, and exhibits a discriminating enthusiasm for one of the most fascinating of novelists.'—*Saturday Review.*

'Seldom has it been our lot to meet with a more appreciative delineation of character than this Memoir of Hawthorne. . . . Mr. Page deserves the best thanks of every admirer of Hawthorne for the way in which he has gathered together these relics, and given them to the world, as well as for his admirable portraiture of their author's life and character.'—*Morning Post.*

'We sympathise very heartily with an effort of Mr. H. A. Page to make English readers better acquainted with the life and character of Nathaniel Hawthorne. . . . He has done full justice to the fine character of the author of "The Scarlet Letter."'—*Standard.*

'He has produced a well-written and complete Memoir. . . A model of literary work of art.'—*Edinburgh Courant.*

XXXV

MEMOIRS OF LEONORA CHRISTINA, Daughter of Christian IV. of Denmark. Written during her imprisonment in the Blue Tower of the Royal Palace at Copenhagen, 1663-1685. Translated by F. E. Bunnett (*Translator of Grimm's 'Life of Michael Angelo' &c.*). With an Autotype Portrait of the Princess. Medium 8vo. 12s. 6d.

A valuable addition to history.'—*Daily News.*

'This remarkable autobiography, in which we gratefully recognise a valuable addition to the tragic romance of history.'—*Spectator.*

XXXVI

LIVES OF ENGLISH POPULAR LEADERS. No. 1. Stephen Langton. By C. Edmund Maurice. Crown 8vo. 7s. 6d.

'Mr. Maurice has written a very interesting book, which may be read with equal pleasure and profit.'—*Morning Post.*

'The volume contains many interesting details, including some important documents. It will amply repay those who read it, whether as a chapter of the constitutional history of England or as the life of a great Englishman.'—*Spectator.*

XXXVII

ECHOES OF A FAMOUS YEAR. By Harriet Parr, Author of 'The Life of Jeanne d'Arc,' 'In the Silver Age,' &c. Crown 8vo. 8s. 6d.

'A graceful and touching, as well as truthful account of the Franco-Prussian War. Those who are in the habit of reading books to children will find this at once instructive and delightful.'—*Public Opinion.*

'Miss Parr has the great gift of charming simplicity of style, and if children are not interested in her book, many of their seniors will be.'—*British Quarterly Review.*

XXXVIII

NORMAN MACLEOD, D.D.: a Contribution towards his Biography. By ALEXANDER STRAHAN. Crown 8vo. sewed. 1s.

* * Reprinted, with numerous Additions and many Illustrations from Sketches by Dr. Macleod, from the *Contemporary Review.*

XXXIX

CABINET PORTRAITS. Biographical Sketches of Living Statesmen. By T. WEMYSS REID. One vol. crown 8vo. 7s. 6d.

'We have never met with a work which we can *more* unreservedly praise. The sketches are absolutely impartial.'—*Athenæum.*

'We can heartily commend his work.'—*Standard.*

'The "Sketches of Statesmen" are drawn with a masterhand.'—*Yorkshire Post.*

XL

THE ENGLISH CONSTITUTION. By WALTER BAGEHOT. A New Edition, revised and corrected, with an Introductory Dissertation on recent changes and events. Crown 8vo. 7s. 6d.

'A pleasing and clever study on the department of higher politics.'—*Guardian.*

'No writer before him had set out so clearly what the efficient part of the English Constitution really is.'—*Pall Mall Gazette.*

'Clear and practical.'—*Globe.*

XLI

REPUBLICAN SUPERSTITIONS. Illustrated by the Political History of the United States. Including a Correspondence with M. Louis Blanc. By MONCURE D. CONWAY. Crown 8vo. 5s.

'Au moment où j'écris ceci, je reçois d'un écrivain très-distingué d'Amérique, M. Conway, une brochure qui est un frappant tableau des maux et des dangers qui résultent aux États-Unis de l'institution présidentielle.'—*M. Louis Blanc.*

'A very able exposure of the most plausible fallacies of Republicanism, by a writer of remarkable vigour and purity of style.'—*Standard.*

XLII

STREAMS FROM HIDDEN SOURCES. By B. MONTGOMERIE RANKING. Crown 8vo. 6s.

XLIII

THE GENIUS OF CHRISTIANITY UNVEILED. Being

Essays by WILLIAM GODWIN, Author of 'Political Justice' &c. Never
before published. One vol, crown 8vo. 7s. 6d.

'Interesting as the frankly expressed thoughts of a remarkable man, and as a
contribution to the history of scepticism.'—*Extract from the Editor's Preface.*

'Few have thought more clearly and directly than William Godwin, or expressed their reflections with more simplicity and unreserve.'—*Examiner.*

'The deliberate thoughts of Godwin deserve to be put before the world for
reading and consideration.'—*Atheneum.*

XLIV

THE PELICAN PAPERS. Reminiscences and Remains of

a Dweller in the Wilderness. By JAMES A. NOBLE. Crown 8vo. 6s.

'Written somewhat after the fashion of Mr. Helps' "Friends in Council."'—
Examiner.

'Will well repay perusal by all thoughtful and intelligent readers.'—*Liverpool Leader.*

'The "Pelican Papers" make a very readable volume.'—*Civilian.*

XLV

SOLDIERING AND SCRIBBLING. By ARCHIBALD FORBES,

of the *Daily News*, Author of 'My Experience of the War between
France and Germany.' Crown 8vo. 7s. 6d.

'All who open it will be inclined to read through, for the varied entertain-
ment which it affords.'—*Daily News.*

'There is a good deal of instruction to outsiders touching military life in this
volume.'—*Evening Standard.*

'There is not a paper in the book which is not thoroughly readable and worth
reading.'—*Scotsman.*

XLVI

BRIEFS AND PAPERS. Being Sketches of the Bar and

the Press. By Two Idle Apprentices. Crown 8vo. 7s. 6d.

'They are written with spirit and knowledge, and give some curious glimpses
into what the majority will regard as strange and unknown territories.'—*Daily
News.*

'This is one of the best books to while away an hour and cause a generous
laugh that we have come across for a long time.'—*John Bull.*

The International Scientific Series.

MESSRS. HENRY S. KING & Co. have the pleasure to announce that under this title they are issuing a SERIES of POPULAR TREATISES, embodying the results of the latest investigations in the various departments of Science at present most prominently before the world.

Although these Works are not specially designed for the instruction of beginners, still, as they are intended to address the *non-scientific public*, they will be, as far as possible, explanatory in character, and free from technicalities. The object of each author will be to bring his subject as near as he can to the general reader.

The volumes will all be crown 8vo. size, well printed on good paper, strongly and elegantly bound, and will sell in this country at a price *not exceeding Five Shillings.*

☞ Prospectuses of the Series may be had of the Publishers.

Already Published,

XLVII

THE FORMS OF WATER IN RAIN AND RIVERS, ICE AND GLACIERS. By J. TYNDALL, LL.D., F.R.S. With 26 Illustrations. Crown 8vo. 5s.

'One of Professor Tyndall's best scientific treatises.'—*Standard.*

'The most recent findings of science and experiment respecting the nature and properties of water in every possible form, are discussed with remarkable brevity, clearness, and fulness of exposition.'—*Graphic.*

'With the clearness and brilliancy of language which have won for him his fame, he considers the subject of ice, snow, and glaciers.'—*Morning Post.*

'Before starting for Switzerland next summer every one should study "The forms of water."'—*Globe.*

'Eloquent and instructive in an eminent degree.'—*British Quarterly.*

XLVIII

PHYSICS AND POLITICS; or, Thoughts on the Application of the Principles of 'Natural Selection' and 'Inheritance' to Political Society. By WALTER BAGEHOT. Crown 8vo. 4s.

'On the whole we can recommend the book as well serving to be read by thoughtful students of politics.'—*Saturday Review.*

'Able and ingenious.'—*Spectator.*

'The book has been well thought out, and the writer speaks without fear.'—*National Reformer.*

'Contains many points of interest, both to the scientific man and to the mere politician.'—*Birmingham Daily Gazette.*

XLIX

ON FOOD. By Dr. EDWARD SMITH, F.R.S. Profusely Illustrated.
Price 5s. [*Just out.*

The Volumes now preparing are—

L

PRINCIPLES OF MENTAL PHYSIOLOGY. With their applications to the Training and Discipline of the Mind, and the Study of its Morbid Conditions. By W. B. CARPENTER, LL.D., M.D., F.R.S., &c. Illustrated.

LI

ANIMAL MECHANICS; or, WALKING, SWIMMING, and FLYING. By Dr. J. BELL PETTIGREW, M.D., F.R.S. 125 Illustrations.

LII

MIND AND BODY: The Theories of their Relations. By ALEXANDER BAIN, LL.D., Professor of Logic at the University of Aberdeen: Illustrated.

LIII

THE STUDY OF SOCIOLOGY. By HERBERT SPENCER.

LIV

THE SECRET OF LONG LIFE. Dedicated by Special Permission to Lord St. Leonards. Second Edition. Large crown 8vo. 6s.

'A charming little volume, written with singular felicity of style and illustration.'—*Times.*

'A very pleasant little book, which is always, whether it deal in paradox or earnest, cheerful, genial, scholarly.'—*Spectator.*

'The bold and striking character of the whole conception is entitled to the warmest admiration.'—*Pall Mall Gazette.*

'We should recommend our readers to get this book . . . . because they will be amused by the jovial, miscellaneous and cultured gossip with which he strews his pages.'—*British Quarterly Review.*

LV

CHANGE OF AIR AND SCENE. A Physician's Hints about Doctors, Patients, Hygiène, and Society; with Notes of Excursions for Health in the Pyrenees, and amongst the Watering-places of France (inland and seaward), Switzerland, Corsica, and the Mediterranean. By Dr. ALPHONSE DONNÉ. Large post 8vo. Price 9s.

'A very readable and serviceable book. . . . . The real value of it is to be found in the accurate and minute information given with regard to a large number of places which have gained a reputation on the Continent for their mineral waters.'—*Pall Mall Gazette.*

'Not only a pleasant book of travel, but also a book of considerable value.'—*Morning Post.*

'A popular account of some of the most charming health resorts of the Continent, with suggestive hints about keeping well and getting well, which are characterised by a good deal of robust common sense.'—*British Quarterly.*

'A singularly pleasant and chatty, as well as instructive, book about health.'—*Guardian.*

'A useful and pleasantly-written book, containing many valuable hints on the general management of health from a shrewd and experienced medical man.'—*Graphic.*

LVI

MISS YOUMANS' FIRST BOOK OF BOTANY. Designed
to Cultivate the Observing Powers of Children. From the Author's
latest Stereotyped Edition. New and Enlarged Edition, with 300
Engravings. Crown 8vo. 5s.

It is but rarely that a school book appears which is at once so novel in plan,
so successful in execution, and so suited to the general want, as to command
universal and unqualified approbation, but such has been the case with Miss
Youmans' First Book of Botany. Her work is an outgrowth of the most recent
scientific views, and has been practically tested by careful trial with juvenile
classes, and it has been everywhere welcomed as a timely and invaluable contribution to the improvement of primary education.

LVII

**AN ESSAY ON THE CULTURE OF THE OBSERVING
POWERS OF CHILDREN,** especially in connection with the Study
of Botany. By ELIZA A. YOUMANS. Edited, with Notes and a Supplement, by JOSEPH PAYNE, F.C.P., Author of 'Lectures on the Science
and Art of Education,' &c. Crown 8vo. 2s. 6d.

'The little book now under notice is expressly designed to make the earliest
instruction of children a mental discipline. Miss Youmans presents in her
work the ripe results of educational experience reduced to a system, wisely
conceiving that an education—even the most elementary—should be regarded
as a discipline of the mental powers, and that the facts of external nature
supply the most suitable materials for this discipline in the case of children.
She has applied that principle to the study of botany. This study, according
to her just notions on the subject, is to be fundamentally based on the exercise
of the pupil's own powers of observation. He is to see and examine the properties of plants and flowers at first hand, not merely to be informed of what
others have seen and examined.'—*Pall Mall Gazette.*

LVIII

THE HISTORY OF THE NATURAL CREATION. Being
a Series of Popular Scientific Lectures on the General Theory of
Progression of Species; with a Dissertation on the Theories of Darwin,
Goethe, and Lamarck; more especially applying them to the Origin
of Man, and to other Fundamental Questions of Natural Science connected therewith. By Professor ERNST HAECKEL, of the University
of Jena. 8vo. With Woodcuts and Plates.

LIX

**AN ARABIC AND ENGLISH DICTIONARY OF THE
KORAN.** By Major J. PENRICE, B.A. 4to. 21s.

LX

MODERN GOTHIC ARCHITECTURE. By T. G. JACKSON.
Crown 8vo. Price 5s.

LXI

A LEGAL HANDBOOK FOR ARCHITECTS. By EDWARD
JENKINS and JOHN RAYMOND. Crown 8vo. Price 5s.

LXII

CONTEMPORARY ENGLISH PSYCHOLOGY. From the
French of Professor TH. RIBOT. An Analysis of the Views and
Opinions of the following Metaphysicians, as expressed in their
writings:

| JAMES MILL. | JOHN STUART MILL. | HERBERT SPENCER. |
| A. BAIN. | GEORGE H. LEWES. | SAMUEL BAILEY. |

Large post 8vo.

LXIII

PHYSIOLOGY FOR PRACTICAL USE. By various
Eminent Writers. Edited by JAMES HINTON. With 50 Illustrations.

LXIV

HEALTH AND DISEASE AS INFLUENCED BY THE
DAILY, SEASONAL, AND OTHER CYCLICAL CHANGES IN THE
HUMAN SYSTEM. By Dr. EDWARD SMITH, F.R.S. A New Edition.
7s. 6d.

LXV

PRACTICAL DIETARY FOR FAMILIES, SCHOOLS, AND
THE LABOURING CLASSES. By Dr. EDWARD SMITH, F.R.S. A
New Edition. Price 3s. 6d.

LXVI

CONSUMPTION IN ITS EARLY AND REMEDIABLE
STAGES. By Dr. EDWARD SMITH, F.R.S. A New Edition. 7s. 6d.

LXVII

IN QUEST OF COOLIES. A South Sea Sketch. By JAMES
L. A. HOPE. Second Edition, crown 8vo. with 15 Illustrations from
Sketches by the Author. Price 6s.

'Mr. Hope's description of the natives is graphic and amusing, and the book
is altogether well worthy of perusal.'—*Standard.*

'Lively and clever sketches.'—*Athenaeum.*

'This agreeably written and amusingly illustrated volume.'—*Public Opinion.*

LXVIII

THE NILE WITHOUT A DRAGOMAN. By FREDERIC EDEN.
Second Edition. In one vol. crown 8vo. cloth, 7s. 6d.

'Should any of our readers care to imitate Mr. Eden's example, and wish to
see things with their own eyes, and shift for themselves, next winter in Upper
Egypt, they will find this book a very agreeable guide.'—*Times.*

'We have in these pages the most minute description of life as it appeared on
the banks of the Nile; all that could be seen or was worth seeing in nature or
in art is here pleasantly and graphically set down. ... It is a book to read
during an autumn holiday.'—*Spectator.*

'Gives, within moderate compass, a suggestive description of the charms,
curiosities, dangers, and discomforts of the Nile voyage.'—*Saturday Review.*

LIX

A TREATISE ON RELAPSING FEVER. By R. T. Lyons, Assistant-Surgeon Bengal Army. Small post 8vo. 7s. 6d.

'A practical work thoroughly supported in its views by a series of remarkable cases.'—*Standard.*

LXX

ROUND THE WORLD IN 1870. A Volume of Travels, with Maps. By A. D. Carlisle, B.A., Trin. Coll., Camb. Demy 8vo. 16s.

'Makes one understand how going round the world is to be done in the quickest and pleasantest manner, and how the brightest and most cheerful of travellers did it with eyes wide open and keen attention all on the alert, with ready sympathies, with the happiest facility of hitting upon the most interesting features of nature and the most interesting characteristics of man, and all for its own sake.'—*Spectator.*

'We can only commend, which we do very heartily, an eminently sensible and readable book.'—*British Quarterly Review.*

MILITARY WORKS.

I

THE FRONTAL ATTACK OF INFANTRY. By Captain Laymann, Instructor of Tactics at the Military College, Neisse. Translated by Colonel Edward Newdigate. Crown 8vo. limp cloth. Price 2s. 6d.

'This work has met with special attention in our army.'—*Militaris Wochenblatt.*

II

THE FIRST BAVARIAN ARMY CORPS IN THE WAR OF 1870-71, UNDER VON DER TANN. Compiled from the Official Records by Capt. Hugo Helvig. Translated by Capt. G. Salis Schwabe. Demy 8vo. With 5 large Maps.

III

History of the Organisation, Equipment, and War Services of

THE REGIMENT OF BENGAL ARTILLERY. Compiled from Published Official and other Records, and various private sources, by Major Francis W. Stubbs, Royal (late Bengal) Artillery. Vol. I. will contain 'War Services.' The second volume will be published separately, and will contain the History of the Organisation and Equipment of the Regiment. In two vols. 8vo. With Maps and Plans. [*Preparing.*

IV

THE ABOLITION OF PURCHASE AND THE ARMY REGULATION BILL OF 1871. By Lieut.-Col. the Hon. A. Anson, V.C., M.P. Crown 8vo. Price 1s.

MILITARY WORKS—(continued.)

v

THE STORY OF THE SUPERSESSIONS. By Lieut.-Col. the Hon. A. Anson, V.C., M.P. Crown 8vo. Price 6d.

vi

ARMY RESERVES AND MILITIA REFORMS. By Lieut.-Col. the Hon. C. Anson. Crown 8vo. sewed, price 1s.

vii

ELEMENTARY MILITARY GEOGRAPHY, RECONNOITRING, AND SKETCHING. Compiled for Non-Commissioned Officers and Soldiers of all Arms. By Lieut. C. E. H. Vincent, Royal Welsh Fusiliers. Small crown 8vo. 2s. 6d.

viii

VICTORIES AND DEFEATS. An attempt to explain the Causes which have led to them. An Officer's Manual. By Col. R. P. Anderson. Demy 8vo. 14s.

ix

STUDIES IN THE NEW INFANTRY TACTICS. By Major W. Von Scherff. Parts I. and II. Translated from the German by Col. Lumley Graham. [Shortly.

x

THE OPERATIONS OF THE FIRST ARMY TO THE CAPITULATION OF METZ. By Major Von Schell, with Maps, including one of Metz and of the country around. Translated by Capt. E. O. Hollist. In demy 8vo.

*** The most important events described in this work are the battles of Spicheren, those before Metz on the 14th and 16th August, and (on this point nothing authentic has yet been published) the history of the investment of Metz (Battle of Noisseville). This work, however, possesses a greater importance than that derived from these points, because it represents for the first time from the official documents the generalship of Von Steinmetz. Hitherto we have had no exact reports on the deeds and motives of this celebrated general. This work has the special object of unfolding carefully the relations in which the commander of the First Army acted, the plan of operations which he drew up, and the manner in which he carried it out.

xi

THE OPERATIONS OF THE FIRST ARMY IN NORTHERN FRANCE AGAINST FAIDHERBE. By Colonel Count Hermann Von Wartensleben, Chief of the Staff of the First Army. Translated by Colonel C. H. Von Wright. In demy 8vo. Uniform with the above.

xii

THE OPERATIONS OF THE FIRST ARMY, UNDER GEN. VON GOEBEN. Translated by Col. C. H. Von Wright. With Maps. Demy 8vo.

MILITARY WORKS—(*continued.*)

XIII

TACTICAL DEDUCTIONS FROM THE WAR OF 1870-1.

By Captain A. VON BOGUSLAWSKI. Translated by Colonel LUMLEY GRAHAM, late 18th (Royal Irish) Regiment. Demy 8vo. Uniform with the above. Price 7s.

'Major Boguslawski's tactical deductions from the war are, that infantry still preserve their superiority over cavalry, that open order must henceforth be the main principles of all drill, and that the chassepot is the best of all small arms for precision. . . . We must, without delay, impress brain and forethought into the British Service; and we cannot commence the good work too soon, or better than by placing the two books ("The Operations of the German Armies" and "Tactical Deductions") we have here criticised in every military library, and introducing them as class-books in every tactical school.' *United Service Gazette.*

XIV

THE OPERATIONS OF THE GERMAN ARMIES IN FRANCE, FROM SEDAN TO THE END OF THE WAR OF 1870-1.

With Large Official Map. From the Journals of the Head-quarters Staff, by Major WM. BLUME. Translated by E. M. JONES, Major 20th Foot, late Professor of Military History, Sandhurst. Demy 8vo. Price 9s.

'The book is of absolute necessity to the military student. . . . The work is one of high merit and . . . has the advantage of being rendered into fluent English, and is accompanied by an excellent military map.'—*United Service Gazette.*

'The work of translation has been well done; the aggressive German idioms have been rendered into clear nervous English without losing any of their original force; and in notes, prefaces, and introductions, much additional information has been given.' *Athenæum.*

'The work of Major von Blume in its English dress forms the most valuable addition to our stock of works upon the war that our press has put forth. Major Blume writes with a clear conscience much wanting in many of his country's historians, and Major Jones has done himself and his original alike justice by his vigorous yet correct translation of the excellent volume on which he has laboured. Our space forbids our doing more than commending it earnestly as the most authentic and instructive narrative of the second section of the war that has yet appeared.'—*Saturday Review.*

XV

THE OPERATIONS OF THE SOUTH ARMY in JANUARY and FEBRUARY 1871.

Compiled from the Official War Documents of the Head-quarters of the Southern Army. By Count HERMANN VON WARTENSLEBEN, Colonel in the Prussian General Staff. Translated by Col. C. H. VON WRIGHT. Demy 8vo, with Maps. Uniform with the above. Price 6s.

XVI

HASTY INTRENCHMENTS.

By Colonel A. BRIALMONT. Translated by Lieutenant CHARLES A. EMPSON, R.A. Demy 8vo. Nine plates. Price 6s.

'A valuable contribution to military literature.'—*Athenæum.*

'In seven short chapters it gives plain directions for performing shelter-trenches, with the best method of carrying the necessary tools; and it offers practical illustrations of the use of hasty intrenchments on the field of battle.'— *United Service Magazine.*

'It supplies that which our own text-books give but imperfectly, viz., hints as to how a position can best be strengthened by means . . . of such extemporised intrenchments and batteries as can be thrown up by infantry in the space of four or five hours . . . deserves to become a standard military work.' *Standard.*

'A clever treatise, short, practical, and clear.'—*Iarrators' Guardian.*
'Clearly and critically written.'—*Wellington Gazette.*

MILITARY WORKS—(*continued.*)

XVII

**THE ARMY OF THE NORTH-GERMAN CONFEDERA-
TION.** A Brief Description of its Organisation, of the different
Branches of the Service and their 'Rôle' in War, of its Mode of
Fighting, &c. By a PRUSSIAN GENERAL. Translated from the
German by Col. EDWARD NEWDIGATE. Demy 8vo. 5s.

,*, The authorship of this book was erroneously ascribed to the renowned General Von
Moltke, but there can be little doubt that it was written under his immediate inspiration.

XVIII

CAVALRY FIELD DUTY. By Major-General VON MIRUS.
Translated by Captain FRANK S. RUSSELL, 14th (King's) Hussars.
Crown 8vo. limp cloth, 5s.

,*, This is the text-book of instruction in the German cavalry, and comprises all the
details connected with the military duties of cavalry soldiers on service. The translation
is made from a new edition, which contains the modifications introduced consequent on
the experiences of the late war. The great interest that students feel in all the German
Military methods, will, it is believed, render this book especially acceptable at the
present time.

XIX

STUDIES IN LEADING TROOPS. By Col. VON VERDY
DU VERNOIS. An authorised and accurate Translation by Lieutenant
H. J. T. HILDYARD, 71st Foot. Parts I. and II. Demy 8vo. 7s.

[*Now ready.*

,*, Gen. BEAUCHAMP WALKER says of this work:—' I recommend the first two numbers
of Colonel von Verdy's "Studies" to the attentive perusal of my brother officers. They
supply a want which I have often felt during my service in this country, namely, a
minuter tactical detail of the minor operations of the war than any but the most observant
and fortunately placed staff officer is in a position to give. I have read and re-read them
very carefully. I hope with profit, certainly with great interest, and believe that practice,
in the sense of them "Studies," would be a valuable preparation for manoeuvre on a
more extended scale.' Berlin, June 1871.

XX

THE FRANCO-GERMAN WAR, 1870-71. First part:
History of the War to the Downfall of the Empire. First Section:
The Events in July. Authorised Translation from the German
Official Account at the Topographical and Statistical Department of
the War Office, by Captain F. C. H. CLARKE, R.A. First Section,
with Map. Demy 8vo. 3s.

XXI

DISCIPLINE AND DRILL. Four Lectures delivered to the
London Scottish Rifle Volunteers. By Captain S. FLOOD PAGE. A
New and Cheaper Edition. Price 1s.

' One of the best-known and clearest-headed of the metropolitan regiments, whose
adjutant, moreover, has lately published an admirable collection of lectures addressed by
him to the men of his corps.'—*Times.*

' The very useful and interesting work. . . . Every Volunteer, officer or private, will
be the better for perusing and digesting the plain-spoken truths which Captain Page so
timely, and yet so modestly, puts before them; and we trust that the little book in which
they are contained will find its way into all parts of Great Britain.'—*Volunteer Service
Gazette.*

XLII

THE SUBSTANTIVE SENIORITY ARMY LIST. Majors
and Captains. By Captain F. B. P. WHITE, 1st W. I. Regiment.
8vo. sewed, 2s. 6d.

BOOKS ON INDIAN SUBJECTS.

I

THE EUROPEAN IN INDIA. A Handbook of Practical
Information for those proceeding to, or residing in, the East Indies,
relating to Outfits, Routes, Time for Departure, Indian Climate, &c.
By EDMUND C. P. HULL. With a Medical Guide for Anglo-Indians.
Being a Compendium of Advice to Europeans in India, relating to
the Preservation and Regulation of Health. By R. S. MAIR, M.D.,
F.R.C.S.E., late Deputy Coroner of Madras. In one vol. post 8vo. 6s.

'Full of all sorts of useful information to the English settler or traveller in
India.'—*Standard.*

'One of the most valuable books ever published in India—valuable for its
sound information, its careful array of pertinent facts, and its sterling common
sense. It is a publisher's as well as an author's "hit," for it supplies a want
which few persons may have discovered, but which everybody will at once
recognise when once the contents of the book have been mastered. The medical part of the work is invaluable.'—*Calcutta Englishman.*

II

EASTERN EXPERIENCES. By L. BOWRING, C.S.I., Lord
Canning's Private Secretary, and for many years the Chief Commis-
sioner of Mysore and Coorg. In one vol. demy 8vo. 16s. Illustrated with Maps and Diagrams.

'An admirable and exhaustive geographical, political, and industrial survey.'
Athenæum.

'The usefulness of this compact and methodical summary of the most authentic information relating to countries whose welfare is intimately connected
with our own should obtain for Mr. Lewin Bowring's work a good place among
treatises of its kind.'—*Daily News.*

'Interesting even to the general reader, but more especially so to those who
may have a special concern in that portion of our Indian Empire.'—*Post.*

'An elaborately got up and carefully compiled work.'—*Home News.*

III

A MEMOIR OF THE INDIAN SURVEYS. By CLEMENT
R. MARKHAM. Printed by order of Her Majesty's Secretary of State
for India in Council. Imperial 8vo. 10s. 6d.

IV

WESTERN INDIA BEFORE and DURING the MUTINIES.
Pictures drawn from Life. By Major-Gen. Sir George le Grand
Jacob, K.C.S.I., C.B. In one vol. crown 8vo. 7s. 6d.

'The most important contribution to the history of Western India during the
Mutinies which has yet, in a popular form, been made public.'—*Athenæum.*

'The legacy of a wise veteran, intent on the benefit of his countrymen rather
than on the acquisition of fame.'—*London and China Express.*

'Few men more competent than himself to speak authoritatively concerning
Indian affairs.'—*Standard.*

V

**EXCHANGE TABLES OF STERLING AND INDIAN
RUPEE CURRENCY,** upon a New and Extended System, embracing
values from One Farthing to One Hundred Thousand Pounds, and at
Rates Progressing, in Sixteenths of a Penny, from 1s. 9d. to 2s. 3d.
per Rupee. By Donald Fraser, Accountant to the British Indian
Steam Navigation Co., Limited. Royal 8vo. 10s. 6d.

VI

**A CATALOGUE of MAPS of the BRITISH POSSESSIONS
IN INDIA AND OTHER PARTS OF ASIA.** Published by order
of Her Majesty's Secretary of State for India in Council. Royal 8vo.
sewed, 1s. A continuation of the above, sewed, price 6d., is now
ready.

☞ Messrs. Henry S. King & Co. are the authorised Agents by the
Government for the Sale of the whole of the Maps enumerated in this
Catalogue.

JUVENILE BOOKS.

I

LOST GIP. By Hesba Stretton, Author of 'Little Meg,'
'Alone in London.' Square crown 8vo. Six Illustrations. Price 1s. 6d.

II

BRAVE MEN'S FOOTSTEPS. A Book of Example and
Anecdote for Young People. By the Editor of 'Men who have Risen.'
With Four Illustrations. By C. Doyle. 3s. 6d.

'The little volume is precisely of the stamp to win the favour of those who, in
choosing a gift for a boy, would consult his moral development as well as his
temporary pleasure.'—*Daily Telegraph.*

'A readable and instructive volume.'—*Examiner.*

'No more welcome book for the schoolboy could be imagined.'—*Birmingham
Daily Gazette.*

JUVENILE BOOKS—(*continued.*)

III

THE LITTLE WONDER-HORN. By JEAN INGELOW. A
Second Series of 'Stories told to a Child.' 15 Illustrations. Cloth,
gilt, 3s. 6d.

 ' Full of fresh and vigorous fancy ; it is worthy of the author of some of the
best of our modern verse.'—*Standard.*
 'We like all the contents of the "Little Wonder-Horn" very much.'—*Athenæum.*
 ' We recommend it with confidence.'—*Pall Mall Gazette.*

IV

STORIES IN PRECIOUS STONES. By HELEN ZIMMERN.
With 6 Illustrations. Crown 8vo. 5s.

 ' A series of pretty tales which are half fantastic, half natural, and pleasantly
quaint, as befits stories intended for the young.'—*Daily Telegraph.*
 'Certainly the book is well worth a perusal, and will not be soon laid down
when once taken up'.—*Daily Bristol Times.*

V

GUTTA-PERCHA WILLIE, THE WORKING GENIUS.
By GEORGE MACDONALD. With Illustrations by ARTHUR HUGHES.
Crown 8vo. 3s. 6d.

VI

THE TRAVELLING MENAGERIE. By CHARLES CAMDEN,
Author of 'Hoity Toity.' Illustrated by J. MAHONEY. Crown 8vo.
3s. 6d.

VII

PLUCKY FELLOWS. A Book for Boys. By STEPHEN J.
MACKENNA. With 6 Illustrations. Crown 8vo. 3s. 6d.

VIII

THE DESERTED SHIP. A Real Story of the Atlantic. By
CUPPLES HOWE, Master Mariner. Illustrated by TOWNLEY GREEN.
Crown 8vo. 3s. 6d.

IX

GOOD WORDS FOR THE YOUNG. The Volume for 1872,
gilt cloth and gilt edges, 7s. 6d. Containing numerous contributions
by popular authors, and about One Hundred and Fifty Illustrations
by the best artists.

X

New Edition.

THE DESERT PASTOR, JEAN JAROUSSEAU. Translated
from the French of EUGÈNE PELLETAN, by Colonel E. P. DE L'HOSTE.
In fcp. 8vo. with an Engraved Frontispiece. Price 3s. 6d.

 ' There is a poetical simplicity and picturesqueness, the noblest heroism, un-
pretentious religion, pure love, and the spectacle of a household brought up in
the fear of the Lord. . . . . The whole story has an air of quaint antiquity
similar to that which invests with a charm more easily felt than described the
site of some splendid ruin.'—*Illustrated London News.*
 ' This charming specimen of Eugène Pelletan's tender grace, humour, and
high-toned morality.'—*Notes and Queries.*
 'A touching record of the struggles in the cause of religious liberty of a real
man.'—*Graphic.*

JUVENILE BOOKS—(continued.)

XI

HOITY TOITY, THE GOOD LITTLE FELLOW. By CHARLES CAMDEN. Illustrated. Crown 8vo. 3s. 6d.

XII

SEEKING HIS FORTUNE, AND OTHER STORIES. Crown 8vo. Six Illustrations.

THE 'ELSIE' SERIES.—PRICE 3s. 6d. EACH.

I

ELSIE DINSMORE. By MARTHA FARQUHARSON. Crown 8vo. Illustrated.

II

ELSIE'S GIRLHOOD: A Sequel to 'Elsie Dinsmore.' By the same Author. Crown 8vo. Illustrated.

III

ELSIE'S HOLIDAYS AT ROSELANDS. By the same Author. Crown 8vo. Illustrated.

POETRY.

I

POT-POURRI. Collected Verses. By AUSTIN DOBSON. Crown 8vo.

II

IMITATIONS FROM THE GERMAN OF SPITTA AND TERSTEGEN. By Lady DURAND. Crown 8vo. 4s. 6d.

III

EASTERN LEGENDS AND STORIES IN ENGLISH VERSE. By Lieutenant NORTON POWLETT, Royal Artillery. Crown 8vo. 5s.

POETRY—(*continued.*)

IV

EDITH; OR, LOVE AND LIFE IN CHESHIRE. By T.
ASHE, Author of the 'Sorrows of Hypsipylé,' &c. Sewed, 6d.

'A really fine poem, full of tender, subtle touches of feeling.'—*Manchester News.*

'Pregnant from beginning to end with the results of careful observation and imaginative power.'—*Chester Chronicle.*

V

THE GALLERY OF PIGEONS, AND OTHER POEMS.
By THEOPHILUS MARZIALS. Crown 8vo. 4s. 6d.

VI

A NEW VOLUME OF SONNETS. By the Rev. C. TENNYSON
TURNER. Crown 8vo. 4s. 6d.

VII

ENGLISH SONNETS. Collected and Arranged by JOHN
DENNIS. Small crown 8vo.

VIII

GOETHE'S FAUST. A New Translation in Rhyme. By the
Rev. C. KEGAN PAUL. Crown 8vo. 6s.

IX

WILLIAM CULLEN BRYANT'S POEMS. Handsomely
Bound. With Illustrations.
A Cheaper Edition.
A Pocket Edition.

X

CALDERON'S DRAMAS. The Purgatory of St. Patrick—The
Wonderful Magician—Life is a Dream. Translated from the Spanish,
by DENIS FLORENCE MACCARTHY.

XI

SONGS FOR SAILORS. By Dr. W. C. BENNETT. Dedicated
by Special Request to H.R.H. the Duke of Edinburgh. Crown 8vo.
3s. 6d. With Steel Portrait and Illustrations.
An Edition in Illustrated Paper Covers. Price 1s.

XII

DR. W. C. BENNETT'S POEMS will be shortly Re-issued,
with additions to each part, in Five Parts, at 1s. each.

XIII

WALLED IN, AND OTHER POEMS. By the Rev. HENRY
J. BULKELY. Crown 8vo. 5s.

POETRY—(*continued.*)

XIV

THE POETICAL AND PROSE WORKS OF ROBERT
BUCHANAN. Preparing for publication, a Collected Edition, in
5 vols.

CONTENTS OF VOL. I.
Daughters of Eve;
Undertones and Antiques;
Country and Pastoral Poems.

XV

SONGS OF LIFE AND DEATH. By JOHN PAYNE, Author
of 'Intaglios,' 'Sonnets,' 'The Masque of Shadows,' &c. Crown
8vo. 6s.

XVI

SONGS OF TWO WORLDS. By a NEW WRITER. Second
Edition. Fcp. 8vo. cloth, 6s.

'The "New Writer" is certainly no tyro. No one after reading the first two
poems, almost perfect in rhythm and all the graceful reserve of true lyrical
strength, can doubt that this book is the result of lengthened thought and
assiduous training in poetical form. . . . . These poems will assuredly take
high rank among the class to which they belong.'—*British Quarterly Review,*
April 1.

'If these poems are the mere preludes of a mind growing in power and in
inclination for verse, we have in them the promise of a fine poet. . . . The
verse describing Socrates has the highest note of critical poetry.'—*Spectator,*
February 17.

'No extracts could do justice to the exquisite tones, the felicitous phrasing,
and delicately wrought harmonies of some of these poems.'—*Nonconformist,*
March 27.

'Are we in this book making the acquaintance of a fine and original poet, or
of a most artistic imitator? And our deliberate opinion is, that the former hypo-
thesis is the right one. It has a purity and delicacy of feeling like morning
air.'—*Graphic, March* 16.

XVII

THE INN OF STRANGE MEETINGS, AND OTHER
POEMS. By MORTIMER COLLINS. Crown 8vo. 6s.

'Abounding in quiet humour, in bright fancy, in sweetness and melody of expression, and, at times, in the tenderest touches of pathos.'—*Graphic.*

'Mr. Collins has an undercurrent of chivalry and romance beneath the trifling
vein of good-humoured banter which is the special characteristic of his verse.
. . . The "Inn of Strange Meetings" is a sprightly piece.'—*Athenæum.*

XVIII

EROS AGONISTES. By E. B. D. Crown 8vo. 3s. 6d.

'The author of these verses has written a very touching story of the human
heart, in the story he tells with such pathos and power, of an affection cherished
so long and so secretly. . . . . It is not the least merit of these pages that
they are everywhere illumined with moral and religious sentiment, suggested,
not paraded, of the brightest, purest character.'—*Standard.*

POETRY—*(continued.)*

XIX

THE LEGENDS OF ST. PATRICK, AND OTHER POEMS.
By AUBREY DE VERE. Crown 8vo. 5s.

'Mr. De Vere's versification in his earlier poems is characterised by great sweetness and simplicity. He is master of his instrument, and rarely offends the ear with false notes. Poems such as these scarcely admit of quotation, for their charm is not, and ought not to be, found in isolated passages ; but we can promise the patient and thoughtful reader much pleasure in the perusal of this volume.'—*Pall Mall Gazette.*

'We have marked in almost every page, excellent touches from which we know not how to select. We have but space to commend the varied structure of his verse, the carefulness of his grammar, and his excellent English. All who believe that poetry should raise and not debase the social ideal—all who think that wit should exalt our standard of thought and manners—must welcome this contribution at once to our knowledge of the past and to the science of noble life.'—*Saturday Review.*

XX

ASPROMONTE, AND OTHER POEMS. Second Edition.
Cloth, 4s. 6d.

'The volume is anonymous, but there is no reason for the author to be ashamed of it. The "Poems of Italy" are evidently inspired by genuine enthusiasm in the cause espoused ; and one of them, "The Execution of Felice Orsini," has much poetic merit, the event celebrated being told with dramatic force.'—*Athenæum.*

'The verse is fluent and free.'—*Spectator.*

XXI

THE DREAM AND THE DEED, AND OTHER POEMS.
By PATRICK SCOTT, Author of 'Footpaths between Two Worlds,' &c. Fcp. 8vo. cloth, 5s.

'A bitter and able satire on the vice and follies of the day—literary, social, and political.'—*Standard.*

'Shows real poetic power coupled with evidences of satirical energy.'—*Edinburgh Daily Review.*

FICTION.

I

BRESSANT. A Romance. By JULIAN HAWTHORNE. 2 vols. crown 8vo.

II

EFFIE'S GAME: How she Lost and How she Won. By CECIL CLAYTON. 2 vols.

III

WHAT 'TIS TO LOVE. By the Author of 'Flora Adair,' 'The Value of Fosterstown.' 3 vols.

FICTION—*(continued.)*

IV

CHESTERLEIGH. By ANSLEY CONYERS. 3 vols. crown 8vo.

V

SQUIRE SILCHESTER'S WHIM. By MORTIMER COLLINS, Author of 'Marquis and Merchant,' 'The Princess Clarice,' &c. 3 vols. crown 8vo.

'We think it the best (story) Mr. Collins has yet written.'—*Pall Mall Gazette.*

VI

SEETA. By Colonel MEADOWS TAYLOR, Author of 'Tara,' 'Ralph Darnell,' &c. 3 vols. crown 8vo.

'The story is well told, native life is admirably described, and the petty intrigues of native rulers, and their hatred of the English, mingled with fear lest the latter should eventually prove the victors, are cleverly depicted.'—*Athenæum.*

'We cannot speak too highly of Colonel Meadows Taylor's book. . . . We would recommend all novel-readers to purchase it at the earliest opportunity.'—*John Bull.*

'Thoroughly interesting and enjoyable reading.'—*Examiner.*

VII

A New and Cheaper Edition, in 1 vol., each Illustrated, price 6s., of -

COL. MEADOWS TAYLOR'S INDIAN TALES is preparing for publication.

The First Volume will be 'THE CONFESSIONS OF A THUG.'

VIII

JOHANNES OLAF. By E. DE WILLE. Translated by F. E. BUNNETT. 3 vols. crown 8vo.

The author of this story enjoys a high reputation in Germany ; and both English and German critics have spoken in terms of the warmest praise of this and her previous stories. She has been called 'The George Eliot' of Germany.

'The book gives evidence of considerable capacity in every branch of a novelist's faculty. The art of description is fully exhibited ; perception of character and capacity for delineating it are obvious ; while there is great breadth and comprehensiveness in the plan of the story.'—*Morning Post.*

IX

OFF THE SKELLIGS. By JEAN INGELOW. (Her First Romance.) In 4 vols. crown 8vo.

'Clever and sparkling. . . . . The descriptive passages are bright with colour.'—*Standard.*

'We read each succeeding volume with increasing interest, going almost to the point of wishing there was a fifth.'—*Athenæum.*

'The novel as a whole is a remarkable one, because it is uncompromisingly true to life.'—*Daily News.*

FICTION—(*continued.*)

x

HONOR BLAKE: The Story of a Plain Woman. By Mrs. KRATINOR, Author of 'English Homes in India' &c. 2 vols. crown 8vo

'One of the best novels we have met with for some time.'—*Morning Post.*

'A story which must do good to all, young and old, who read it.'—*Daily News.*

xi

THE DOCTOR'S DILEMMA. By HESBA STRETTON, Author of 'Little Meg' &c. 3 vols. crown 8vo.

xii

THE PRINCESS CLARICE. A Story of 1871. By MORTIMER COLLINS. 2 vols. crown 8vo.

'Mr. Collins has produced a readable book, amusingly characteristic. There is good description of Devonshire scenery ; and lastly, there is Clarice, a most successful heroine, who must speak to the reader for herself.'—*Athenæum.*

'Very readable and amusing. We would especially give an honourable mention to Mr. Collins's "revs de société," the writing of which has almost become a lost art.'—*Pall Mall Gazette.*

'A bright, fresh, and original book, with which we recommend all genuine novel readers to become acquainted at the earliest opportunity.'—*Standard.*

xiii

A GOOD MATCH. By AMELIA PERRIER, Author of 'Mea Culpa.' 2 vols.

'Racy and lively.'—*Athenæum.*

'As pleasant and readable a novel as we have seen this season.'—*Examiner.*

'This clever and amusing novel.'—*Pall Mall Gazette.*

'Agreeably written.'—*Public Opinion.*

xiv

THE SPINSTERS OF BLATCHINGTON. By MAR. TRAVERS. 2 vols. crown 8vo.

'A pretty story. Deserving of a favourable reception.'—*Graphic.*

'A book of more than average merit—worth reading.'—*Examiner.*

xv

THOMASINA. By the Author of 'Dorothy,' 'De Cressy,' &c. 2 vols. crown 8vo.

'A finished and delicate cabinet picture ; no line is without its purpose, but all contribute to the unity of the work.'—*Athenæum.*

'For the delicacies of character-drawing, for play of incident, and for finish of style, we must refer our readers to the story itself.'—*Daily News.*

This undeniably pleasing story.'—*Pall Mall Gazette.*

FICTION—*(continued.)*

XVI

THE STORY OF SIR EDWARD'S WIFE. By HAMILTON MARSHALL, Author of ' For Very Life.' 1 vol. crown 8vo.

' A quiet, graceful little story.'—*Spectator.*
' There are many clever conceits in it . . . Mr. Hamilton Marshall can tell story closely and pleasantly.'—*Pall Mall Gazette.*

XVII

LINKED AT LAST. By F. E. BUNNETT. 1 vol. crown 8vo.

' " Linked at Last " contains so much of pretty description, natural incident, and delicate portraiture, that the reader who once takes it up will not be inclined to relinquish it without concluding the volume.'—*Morning Post.*
' A very charming story.'—*John Bull.*

XVIII

PERPLEXITY. By SYDNEY MOSTYN. 3 vols. crown 8vo.

' Written with very considerable power . . . original . . . worked out with great cleverness and sustained interest.'—*Standard.*
' Shows much lucidity—much power of portraiture.'—*Examiner.*
' Forcibly and graphically told.'—*Daily News.*
' Written with very considerable power, the plot is original and worked out with great cleverness and sustained interest.'—*Standard.*
' Shows much lucidity, much power of portraiture, and no inconsiderable sense of humour.'—*Examiner.*
' The literary workmanship is good, and the story forcibly and graphically told.'—*Daily News.*

XIX

HER TITLE OF HONOUR. By HOLME LEE. Second Edition. 1 vol. crown 8vo.

' With the interest of a pathetic story is united the value of a definite and high purpose.'—*Spectator.*
' A most exquisitely written story.'—*Literary Churchman.*

XX

CRUEL AS THE GRAVE. By the Countess VON BOTHMER. 3 vols. crown 8vo.

' *Jealousy is cruel as the Grave.*'

' An interesting, though somewhat tragic story.'—*Athenæum.*
' An agreeable, unaffected, and eminently readable novel.'—*Daily News.*

XXI

MEMOIRS OF MRS. LETITIA BOOTHBY. By WILLIAM CLARK RUSSELL, Author of 'The Book of Authors.' Crown 8vo. 7s. 6d.

' The book is clever and ingenious.'—*Saturday Review.*
' One of the most delightful books I have read for a very long while. Very few works of truth or fiction are so thoroughly entertaining from the first page to the last.'—*Judy.*
' This is a very clever book, one of the best imitations of the productions of the last century that we have seen.'—*Guardian.*

FICTION—(*continued.*)

XXII

LITTLE HODGE. A Christmas Country Carol. By EDWARD
JENKINS, Author of 'Ginx's Baby,' &c. Illustrated. Crown 8vo. 5s.
A Cheap Edition in paper covers, price 1s.

'We shall be mistaken if it does not obtain a very wide circle of readers.'—
United Service Gazette.

'Wise and humorous, but yet most pathetic.'—*Nonconformist.*

'The pathos of some of the passages is extremely touching.'—*Manchester
Examiner.*

'One of the most seasonable of Christmas stories.'—*Literary World.*

XXIII

GINX'S BABY: HIS BIRTH AND OTHER MISFORTUNES.
By EDWARD JENKINS. Twenty-ninth Edition. Crown 8vo. 2s.

XXIV

LORD BANTAM. By EDWARD JENKINS, Author of 'Ginx's
Baby.' Sixth Edition. Crown 8vo. 2s.

XXV

HERMANN AGHA. An Eastern Narrative. By W. GIFFORD
PALGRAVE, Author of 'Travels in Central Arabia,' &c. Second
Edition. 2 vols. crown 8vo. cloth, extra gilt, 18s.

'Reads like a tale of life, with all its incidents: the young will take to it for
its love portions, the older for its descriptions, some in this day for its Arab
philosophy.'—*Athenæum.*

'The cardinal merit, however, of the story is, to our thinking, the exquisite
simplicity and purity of the love portion. There is a positive fragrance as of
newly-mown hay about it, as compared with the artificially perfumed passions
which are detailed to us with such gusto by our ordinary novel-writers in their
endless volumes.'—*Observer.*

XXVI

SEPTIMIUS. A Romance. By NATHANIEL HAWTHORNE,
Author of 'The Scarlet Letter,' 'Transformation,' &c. Second Edition.
1 vol. crown 8vo. cloth, extra gilt, 9s.

A peculiar interest attaches to this work. It was the last thing the author
wrote, and he may be said to have died as he finished it.

The *Athenæum* says that 'the book is full of Hawthorne's most characteristic
writing.'

'One of the best examples of Hawthorne's writing; every page is impressed
with his peculiar view of thought, conveyed in his own familiar way.'—*Post.*

XXVII

PANDURANG HARI; or, Memoirs of a Hindoo. A Tale
of Mahratta Life Sixty Years ago. With a Preface by Sir H. BARTLE
E. FRERE, G.C.S.I. &c. 2 vols. crown 8vo. 21s.

XXVIII

THE TASMANIAN LILY. By JAMES BONWICK, Author of
'Curious Facts of Old Colonial Days' &c. Crown 8vo. Illustrated, 5s.

THE
CORNHILL LIBRARY OF FICTION.
3s. 6d. per Volume.

It is intended in this Series to produce books of such merit that readers will care to preserve them on their shelves. They are well printed on good paper, handsomely bound, with a Frontispiece, and are sold at the moderate price of 3s. 6d. each.

I

ROBIN GRAY. By CHARLES GIBBON. With a Frontispiece by HENNESSY.

II

KITTY. By Miss M. BETHAM-EDWARDS.

III

READY MONEY MORTIBOY. A Matter-of-Fact Story.

IV

HIRELL. By JOHN SAUNDERS, Author of 'Abel Drake's Wife.'

V

ONE OF TWO. By J. HAIN FRISWELL, Author of 'The Gentle Life' &c.

VI

GOD'S PROVIDENCE HOUSE. By Mrs. G. L. BANKS.
Other Standard Novels to follow.

FORTHCOMING NOVELS.

I

CIVIL SERVICE. By J. T. LISTADO, Author of 'Maurice Reynhart.' 2 vols.

II

VANESSA. By the Author of 'Thomasina,' &c.   2 vols.

III

A LITTLE WORLD. By GEO. MANVILLE FENN, Author of 'The Sapphire Cross,' 'Mad,' &c.

IV

TOO LATE. By Mrs NEWMAN.   2 vols. crown 8vo.

V

THE QUEEN'S SHILLING. By Capt. ARTHUR GRIFFITHS, Author of 'Peccavi; or, Geoffrey Singleton's Mistake.' 2 vols.

VI

TWO GIRLS. By FREDK. WEDMORE, Author of 'A Snapt Gold Ring.' 2 vols. crown 8vo.

FORTHCOMING NOVELS—*(continued.)*

VII

MIRANDA: A Midsummer Madness. By MORTIMER COLLINS.

VIII

HEATHERGATE. In 2 vols.

THEOLOGICAL.

I

HYMNS AND VERSES. Original and Translated. By the
Rev. HENRY DOWNTON. Small crown 8vo.

II

THE ETERNAL LIFE. Being Fourteen Sermons. By the
Rev. JAMES NOBLE BENNIE, M.A. Crown 8vo. 6s.

III

MISSIONARY ENTERPRISE IN THE EAST. By the Rev.
RICHARD COLLINS. Illustrated. Crown 8vo. 6s.

IV

THE REALM OF TRUTH. By Miss E. CARNE. Crown 8vo
6s. 6d.

V

HYMNS FOR THE CHURCH AND HOME. By the Rev.
W. FLEMING STEVENSON, Author of 'Praying and Working.'

VI

**THE YOUNG LIFE EQUIPPING ITSELF FOR GOD'S
SERVICE.** Being Four Sermons preached before the University of
Cambridge in November 1872. By the Rev. J. C. VAUGHAN, D.D.,
Master of the Temple. Third Edition. Crown 8vo. 3s. 6d.

VII

WORDS AND WORKS IN A LONDON PARISH. Edited
by the Rev. CHARLES ANDERSON, M.A. Demy 8vo. 6s.

VIII

LIFE. Conferences delivered at Toulouse. By the Rev. PÈRE
LACORDAIRE. Crown 8vo. 6s.

IX

THOUGHTS FOR THE TIMES. By the Rev. H. R. HAWEIS,
M.A., Author of 'Music and Morals,' &c. Third Edition. Crown
8vo. 7s. 6d.

X

CATHOLICISM AND THE VATICAN. With a Narrative of
the Old Catholic Congress at Munich. By J. LOWRY WHITTLE, A.M.,
Trin. Coll., Dublin. Second Edition. Crown 8vo. 7s. 6d.

' A valuable and philosophic contribution to the solution of one of the greatest
questions of this stirring age.'—*Church Times.*

' We cannot follow the author through his graphic and lucid sketch of the
Catholic movement in Germany and of the Munich Congress, at which he was
present; but we may cordially recommend his book to all who wish to follow
the course of the movement.'—*Saturday Review.*

THEOLOGICAL—(continued.)

XI

NAZARETH: ITS LIFE AND LESSONS. By the Rev.
G. S. Drew, Vicar of Trinity, Lambeth. Second Edition. In small
8vo. cloth, 5s.

'*In Him was life, and the life was the light of men.*'

'A singularly reverent and beautiful book; the style in which it is written is not less chaste and attractive than its subject.'—*Daily Telegraph.*

'Perhaps one of the most remarkable books recently issued in the whole range of English theology. . . . Original in design, calm and appreciative in language, noble and elevated in style, this book, we venture to think, will live.'—*Churchman's Magazine.*

XII

**SCRIPTURE LANDS IN CONNECTION WITH THEIR
HISTORY.** By G. S. Drew, M.A., Vicar of Trinity, Lambeth; Author
of 'Reasons of Faith.' Second Edition. Bevelled boards, 8vo. price
10s. 6d.

'Mr. Drew has invented a new method of illustrating Scripture history—from observation of the countries. Instead of narrating his travels, and referring from time to time to the facts of sacred history belonging to the different countries, he writes an outline history of the Hebrew nation from Abraham downwards, with special reference to the various points in which the geography illustrates the history. The advantages of this plan are obvious. Mr. Drew thus gives us not a mere imitation of "Sinai and Palestine," but a view of the same subject from the other side. . . . He is very successful in picturing to his readers the scenes before his own mind. The position of Abraham in Palestine is portrayed, both socially and geographically, with great vigour. Mr. Drew has given an admirable account of the Hebrew sojourn in Egypt, and has done much to popularise the newly-acquired knowledge of Assyria in connection with the two Jewish Kingdoms.'—*Saturday Review.*

XIII

MEMORIES OF VILLIERSTOWN. By C. J. S. Crown 8vo.
With Frontispiece. 5s.

XIV

SIX PRIVY COUNCIL JUDGMENTS — 1850-1872. Anno-
tated by W. G. Brooke, M.A., Barrister-at-Law. Crown 8vo. 9s.

XV

**THE DIVINE KINGDOM ON EARTH AS IT IS IN
HEAVEN.** By the Author of 'Nazareth: its Life and Lessons.' In
demy 8vo. bound in cloth, 10s. 6d. [*Now ready.*

'*Our Commonwealth is in Heaven.*'

'A high purpose and a devout spirit characterise this work. It is thoughtful and eloquent. . . . The most valuable and suggestive chapter is entitled "Fulfilment in Life and Ministry of Christ," which is full of original thinking admirably expressed.'—*British Quarterly Review.*

'It is seldom that, in the course of our critical duties, we have to deal with a volume of any size or pretension so entirely valuable and satisfactory as this. Published anonymously as it is, there is no living divine to whom the authorship would not be a credit. . . . Not the least of its merits is the perfect simplicity and clearness conjoined with a certain massive beauty of its style.'—*Literary Churchman.*

THEOLOGICAL—(continued.)

LIFE AND WORKS OF THE REV. FRED. W. ROBERTSON.
New and Cheaper Editions.

LIFE and LETTERS. Edited by Stopford Brooke, M.A., Chaplain in Ordinary to the Queen.

In 2 vols. uniform with the Sermons. 7s. 6d.

Library Edition, in demy 8vo. with Two Steel Portraits. 12s.

A Popular Edition, in 1 vol. 6s.

SERMONS. Four Series. 4 vols. small crown 8vo. 3s. 6d. per vol.

EXPOSITORY LECTURES ON ST. PAUL'S EPISTLE TO THE CORINTHIANS. Small crown 8vo. 5s.

AN ANALYSIS OF MR. TENNYSON'S 'In Memoriam.' (Dedicated by permission, to the Poet-Laureate.) Fcp. 8vo. 2s.

The **EDUCATION of the HUMAN RACE.** Translated from the German of Gotthold Ephraim Lessing. Fcp. 8vo. 2s. 6d.

LECTURES AND ADDRESSES ON LITERARY AND SOCIAL TOPICS. Small crown 8vo. 3s. 6d. [*Preparing.*]

A **LECTURE ON FRED. W.** ROBERTSON, M.A. By the Rev. F. A. Noble. Delivered before the Young Men's Christian Association of Pittsburgh, U.S. 1s. 6d.

SERMONS BY THE REV. STOPFORD A. BROOKE, M.A.
Chaplain in Ordinary to Her Majesty the Queen.

CHRIST IN MODERN LIFE. Sermons preached in St. James's Chapel, York Street, London. Third Edition. Crown, 8vo. 7s. 6d.

'Nobly fearless and singularly strong . . . carries our admiration throughout.'—*British Quarterly Review.*

FREEDOM IN THE CHURCH OF ENGLAND. Six Sermons suggested by the Voysey Judgment. Second Edition. In 1 vol. crown 8vo. cloth, 3s. 6d.

'A very fair statement of the views in respect to freedom of thought held by the Liberal party in the Church of England.'—*Blackwood's Magazine.*

'Interesting and readable, and characterised by great clearness of thought, frankness of statement, and moderation of tone.'—*Church Opinion.*

SERMONS. Preached in St. James's Chapel, York Street, London. Sixth Edition. Crown 8vo. 6s.

'No one who reads these sermons will wonder that Mr. Brooke is a great power in London, that his chapel is thronged, and his followers large and enthusiastic. They are fiery, energetic, impetuous sermons, rich with the treasures of a cultivated imagination.'—*Guardian.*

THE LIFE AND WORK OF FREDERICK DENISON MAURICE. A Memorial Sermon. Crown 8vo. sewed, 1s.

THE DAY OF REST.

Weekly, price One Penny, and in Monthly Parts, price Sixpence.

Among the leading Contributions to the first year's issue may be mentioned:—

Words for the Day. By C. J. Vaughan, D.D., Master of the Temple.

Labours of Love: being further Accounts of what is being done by Dr. Wichern and others. By the Rev. W. Fleming Stevenson, Author of 'Praying and Working.'

Occasional Papers. By the Rev. Thomas Binney.

Sundays in my Life. By the Author of 'Episodes in an Obscure Life.'

Songs of Rest. By George Macdonald.

To Rome and Back. A Narrative of Personal Experience. By One who has made the Journey.

. The late Dr. Norman Macleod, during the last few months of his life, frequently urged the preparation of a series of Popular Papers, by a thoroughly competent person, on the Church of Rome as it really is to-day. 'To Rome and Back' is the result of his suggestion.

The Battle of the Poor: Sketches from Courts and Alleys. By Hesba Stretton, Author of 'Jessica's First Prayer,' and 'Little Meg's Children.'

Illustrated by the best Artists.

Price One Penny Weekly. Monthly Parts, Price Sixpence.

THE CONTEMPORARY REVIEW.
THEOLOGICAL, LITERARY, AND SOCIAL.
Price Half-a-Crown Monthly.

THE SAINT PAULS MAGAZINE.
LIGHT AND CHOICE.
Price One Shilling Monthly.

GOOD THINGS FOR THE YOUNG OF ALL AGES.

Edited by George Macdonald.

And Illustrated by the best Artists.

Price Sixpence Monthly.

IMPORTANT MILITARY WORKS.

THE OPERATIONS OF THE GERMAN ARMIES IN FRANCE, FROM SEDAN TO THE END OF THE WAR OF 1870-71. With large Official Map. From the Journals of the Head-quarters Staff. By Major WM. BLUME. Translated by E. M. JONES, Major 20th Foot, late Professor of Military History, Sandhurst. Demy 8vo. Price 9s.

"The book is of absolute necessity to the military student. . . . The work is one of high merit, and has the advantage of being rendered into clear English, and is accompanied by an excellent military map."—*United Service Gazette.*

"The work of translation has been well done; the expressive German idioms have been rendered into clear nervous English, without losing any of their original force; and in notes, prefaces, and introductions, much additional information has been given."—*Athenæum.*

"The work of Major von Blume in its English dress form the most valuable addition to our stock of works upon the war that our press has put forth. Major Blume writes with a clear conciseness much wanting in many of his country's historians, and Major Jones has done himself and his original alike justice by his vigorous yet correct translation of the excellent volume on which he has laboured, this space forbids our doing more than commending it earnestly as the most authentic and instructive narrative of the second section of the war that has yet appeared."—*Saturday Review.*

THE OPERATIONS OF THE SOUTH ARMY IN JANUARY AND FEBRUARY, 1871. Compiled from the Official War Documents of the Head-quarters of the Southern Army. By Count HERMANN VON WARTENSLEBEN, Colonel in the Prussian General Staff. Translated by Colonel C. H. VON WRIGHT. Demy 8vo. With Maps. Uniform with the above. Price 6s.

THE OPERATIONS OF THE FIRST ARMY TO THE CAPITULATION OF METZ. By Major VON SCHELL, with Maps, including one of Metz and of the country around. Translated by Capt. E. O. HOLLIST. In demy 8vo.

"*The most important events described in this work are the battles of Spichern, those before Metz on the 15th and 18th August, and (on this point nothing authentic has yet been published) the history of the investment of Metz from the side of Noisseville. This work, however, possesses a greater importance than that derived from these points, because it represents for the first time from the official documents the generalship of Von Steinmetz. Hitherto we have had no exact reports on the deeds and motives of this celebrated general. This work has the special object of unfolding carefully the relations in which the commander of the First Army acted, the plan of operations which he drew up, and the manner in which he carried it out.*

THE OPERATIONS OF THE FIRST ARMY IN NORTHERN FRANCE AGAINST FAIDHERBE. By Colonel Count HERMANN VON WARTENSLEBEN, Chief of the Staff of the First Army. Translated by Colonel C. H. VON WRIGHT. In demy 8vo. Uniform with the above.

THE OPERATIONS OF THE FIRST ARMY UNDER GENERAL VON GOEBEN. Translated by Col. C. H. VON WRIGHT. With Maps. Demy 8vo. Price 9s.

THE FIRST BAVARIAN ARMY CORPS IN THE WAR OF 1870-71, UNDER VON DER TANN. Compiled from the Official Records by Capt. HUGO HELVIG. Translated by Capt. G. SALIS SCHWABE. Demy 8vo. With 5 large Maps.

TACTICAL DEDUCTIONS FROM THE WAR OF 1870-71. By Captain A. VON BOGUSLAWSKI. Translated by Colonel LUMLEY GRAHAM, late 18th (Royal Irish) Regiment. Demy 8vo. Uniform with the above. Price 7s.

"Major Boguslawski's tactical deductions from the war are, that infantry still preserve their superiority over cavalry, that open order must henceforth be the main principles of all drill, and that fire Chassepôts is the best of all small arms of precision. . . . We need without delay improve brain and forethought into the British Service, and we cannot commence the good work too soon, or better than by placing the two books ['The Operations of the German Armies' and 'Tactical Deductions'] we have here criticised in every military library, and introducing them as class-books in every tactical school."—*United Service Gazette.*

HASTY INTRENCHMENTS. By Colonel A. BRIALMONT. Translated by Lieutenant CHARLES A. EMPSON, R.A. Demy 8vo. Nine Plates. Price 6s.

"A valuable contribution to military literature."—*Athenæum.*

"In seven short chapters it gives plain directions for performing shelter-trenches, with the best method of carrying the necessary tools, and it offers practical illustrations of the use of hasty intrenchments on the field of battle."—*United Service Magazine.*

"It supplies that which our own text-books give but imperfectly, viz., hints as to how a position can best be strengthened by means . . . of such extemporised intrenchments and batteries as can be thrown up by infantry in the space of four or five hours . . . deserves to become a standard military work."—*Standard.*

"A clever treatise, short, practical, and clear."—*Inventor's Guardian.*

"Clearly and critically written."—*Wellington Gazette.*

HENRY S. KING & CO. 65 CORNHILL, AND 12 PATERNOSTER ROW.